Travel Geography for Tourism

Part 1 United Kingdom

Travel Geography for Tourism

Part 1 United Kingdom

Pauline Horner

Stanley Thornes (Publishers) Ltd

First Published in 1993 by:
Stanley Thornes (Publishers) Ltd
Old Station Drive
Leckhampton
Cheltenham GL53 0DN
England

A catalogue record for this book is available from the British Library.
ISBN 0 7487 1557 6

Typeset by Tech-Set, Tyne & Wear.
Printed and bound in Great Britain at The Bath Press, Avon.

Contents

Dedication

I would like to dedicate this book with thanks to my parents Marie and Bill Sharratt who taught me from an early age to love and appreciate many of the attractions described in this book.

Acknowledgements

The author and publishers are grateful to the British Tourist Authority, the English Tourist Board, the Scottish Tourist Board, the Wales Tourist Board and the Northern Ireland Tourist Board for permission to reproduce their logos on page 2.

The authors and publishers are also grateful to the following for the loan of photographs:

Beamish Open Air Museum (page 12); Butlin's (page 13); © Crown, Historic Royal Palaces (page 16); Edinburgh Marketing (page 72); Marian Rees, Snowdonia National Park, Penrhyndeudraeth, Gwynedd (page 85); MetroCentre (page 4); Northern Ireland Tourist Board (page 101); Thorpe Park, Surrey (page 23); Tourism Department, States of Jersey (page 107); Wales Tourist Board (page 93) and Warwick Castle (page 44). All other photographs were supplied by the author.

Introduction

The aim of this book is to provide underpinning geography knowledge and skills appropriate to a variety of qualifications in the British travel industry. Travel courses and qualifications are available from school to University, as well as through training in the workplace.

A full range of National Vocational Qualifications (NVQs) from level 1 to 5 is available, as well as General National Vocational Qualifications (GNVQs), BTEC qualifications at First, National and Higher levels. In addition, City and Guilds offer a variety of examinable qualifications such as:

480 Introduction to Tourism in the UK
482 Visitor Attraction Management
488 Certificate in UK Tourism
489 Visitor Attraction Operations
492 Certificate of Tourist Information Centre Competence
495 Certificate of Travel Agency Competence
499 Certificate in Travel Studies.

GCSE Travel and Tourism is available in many schools and the English Tourist Board sets examinations on UK travel geography, history and architecture for Blue Badge Guides.

All of these qualifications involve underpinning knowledge about, and skills with travel geography.

This is the first of two books on *Travel Geography for Tourism*. Part 1 provides information about UK holiday destinations including London; English, Scottish and Welsh areas; Northern Ireland and the Channel Islands. Part 2 provides information about European and worldwide destinations which are popular with UK tourists. Tried and tested destinations such as Spain and the USA are included, as well as growing markets in Eastern Europe and the Far East.

Each chapter has an activity through which the reader can learn and practise travel geography skills such as:

♦ atlas reading
♦ route planning
♦ itineraries
♦ planning a day excursion
♦ responding to a client's letter
♦ giving informed comparative advice
♦ case studies
♦ presentations
♦ brochure research
♦ using current sources of information.

These underpinning skills are all part of travel geography but are best taught through activities, such as those outlined in the book. During the activities the students should receive guidance from a lecturer or trainer.

The following table indicates the chapters in which appropriate activities can be found. This is included to assist those who wish to learn, or reinforce, a particular travel geography skill.

Travel geography skill	Activity in chapter
atlas reading	1
brochure research	11
case studies	13
giving informed comparative advice	16
planning a day excursion by coach	4
planning a day excursion by public transport	3
planning a familiarisation trip	6
interpretive skills	10
itineraries	8
responding to a client's letter	5
presentations	15
promotional slides or illustrations	7
route planning	12
using current sources of information	2
city walking tour	9
countryside walking tour	14

1 Setting the UK Travel Geography Scene

What is tourism?

In its widest sense we could say that tourism is temporary or short term travel to a place, or places, other than where the person normally lives. If people travel for only a day we call them excursionists or day-trippers, but if they stay one or more nights then we call them tourists. People become tourists or day-trippers for many reasons:

♦ relaxation, pleasure, health, or sport
♦ religious, cultural, educational or historical interests
♦ business
♦ visits to friends and relatives and to meet other people.

Many people become tourists for more than just one of these reasons.

Wherever tourists spend their holidays there are usually certain facilities that they expect, such as:

♦ assistance from a travel agent, or from the reservations staff of the airline, coach company or ferry, to reach their destination.
♦ somewhere to stay, such as a hotel, flatlet or caravan.
♦ a restaurant or cafeteria
♦ information about the place in which they are staying.
♦ some form of entertainment.

Providing these facilities creates jobs in the travel industry for those who are willing to meet the needs of the modern holidaymaker and business traveller. Tourists who are seeking information about the place in which they are staying often make enquiries of their hotel receptionist, coach driver, or waitress in the local cafe as well as through the more traditional sources of information in booking offices, tourist information centres and official guides.

Tourism is big business throughout the world and the UK ranks fourth in the world, after France, Spain and the USA, in terms of international tourism receipts. Tourism is in fact one of the UK's most important industries, earning £25 billion a year, which is more than food manufacture, motor vehicles or aerospace. Tourists in the UK may be:

♦ UK domestic tourists, or
♦ incoming foreign tourists.

UK domestic tourists take over 115 million trips of one night or more each year and to this can be added the numerous day trips taken, usually within a hundred miles of home towns. Overseas visitors account for about 18 per cent of all tourist attraction visits in the UK. Incoming visitors are particularly interested in British heritage and they account for 36 per cent share of visits to historic buildings and 44 per cent of visits to London attractions.

Over a third of incoming tourists arrive from English-speaking nations such as the USA, Canada and Australia and their average length of stay is high in proportion to visitors from the rest of Europe. Seasonality seems to be unimportant, particularly for London, which is regarded as an all-year, all-weather destination. The biggest spenders by far are American and Japanese tourists. From the European market most visitors come from France and Germany.

The importance of tourism to the British economy was recognised in 1969 with the Development of Tourism Act.

Development of Tourism Act 1969

Prior to 1969 there was no clear government policy on tourism in the UK and this often resulted in conflicting and wasteful use of resources. In 1969 the Development of Tourism Act of Parliament established:

- the British Tourist Authority or the BTA, which is concerned with encouraging incoming tourism
- the four Tourist Boards of England, Scotland, Wales and Northern Ireland which are concerned with tourism in their own national areas.

With the passing of this Act, the BTA and the National Tourist Boards were given not only guidelines, but also the power and authority to act in the name of the government and to promote British Tourism with an effective voice.

- The British Tourist Authority employs about 200 staff in over 20 overseas offices. These BTA offices provide information for those who are interested in visiting this country.
- A BTA office can set up workshops or educational tours to bring together British organisations and potential overseas clients.
- One BTA initiative is to help promote training in customer care for staff in the tourist industry. Their training package includes seminars, self-study packs, handbooks and videos all aimed at improving the image we offer to tourists in this country.

Such national initiatives would have been difficult to organise prior to the introduction of the 1969 Development of Tourism Act. The National Tourist Boards are:

- the English Tourist Board (ETB)
- the Scottish Tourist Board (STB)
- the Wales Tourist Board (WTB)
- the Northern Ireland Tourist Board (NITB).

Each Tourist Board works within its own country to encourage the provision and improvement of tourist amenities.

The Tourist Boards were empowered by the 1969 Act to promote publicity and advertising, to offer information services, to undertake research and to provide grants for tourist related projects. The English Tourist Board, along with the British Tourist Authority reports to the Department of Employment, and the Scottish and Wales Tourist Boards are responsible to their respective Secretaries of State.

In order to extend their influence within their countries, the National Tourist Boards set up Regional Tourist Boards and Councils. There are:

- 12 Regional Tourist Boards in England
- 32 Regional Tourist Boards in Scotland
- 3 Regional Councils in Wales.

The Regional Tourist Boards provide Tourist Information Centres (TIC) and offer a variety of publications giving details of local accommodation and places of interest.

Southport Tourist Information Centre

Each National Tourist Board participates in exhibitions and workshops and, in fact, the largest stand at the World Travel Market in London each year is taken by the British Tourist Authority and the National and Regional Tourist Boards. Every year the Boards produce statistical facts, such as the number of visitors to particular attractions in their area, and they constantly undertake surveys and research to update their information.

Diagram 1.1   Map of the 12 English Regional Tourist Board areas

What do tourists do in the UK?

According to a survey of the English Tourist Board, many day-trippers and overseas visitors have shopping at the top of their list. The most popular places for shopping in London are Oxford Street and Regent Street, followed closely by Knightsbridge. The importance of shopping as a tourist activity has been recognised throughout the country with developments such as the Albert Dock in Liverpool and the MetroCentre in Gateshead. The MetroCentre is Europe's largest out-of-town shopping and leisure complex with three miles of tree-lined shopping malls, a fantasy fairground for children and a cinema and bowling centre for all the family. The shopping malls have all the main department stores, over 30 individual trading barrows and three themed areas such as the Antique Village. In the Antique Village at the MetroCentre the architecture, decor and shops are in keeping with the theme of an old fashioned English village green, reminiscent of a chocolate box cover.

Visits to attractions are important to day-trippers, domestic tourists and incoming tourists. A joint survey by the UK Tourist Boards rates the top ten UK tourist attractions as:

- Madame Tussaud's, London
- Alton Towers, Staffordshire
- Tower of London
- Blackpool Tower, Lancashire
- Natural History Museum, London
- Thorpe Park, Surrey
- Chessington World of Adventures, Surrey
- Kew Gardens, London
- Science Museum, London
- Windsor Safari Park, Berkshire.

Statistics for this league table are based on attractions which charge admission and so this list excludes many other very popular attractions such as cathedrals, museums, fairgrounds and countryside. For example, these figures do not take into account visits to English parish churches, many of which are listed buildings. The English Tourist Board estimates that these churches receive at least 12 million visits a year.

Antique village at the MetroCentre, Gateshead, Tyne and Wear

There are nearly 5000 visitor attractions in the UK where attendance, capacity, and admission charges are monitored by the Tourist Boards. The types of attraction vary from historic houses to craft centres, lakes and reservoirs. Diagram 1.2 gives an indication of the types of attraction and their proportional appeal. Museums and art galleries are the most popular, followed closely by historic buildings.

1989 was an exceptionally good summer in the UK and the British Tourist Authority issued figures that year showing comparisons with previous attendance at tourist attractions. Not surprisingly, attendance at wildlife attractions was up by 3 per cent but historic houses received an even greater 4 per cent increase. It would seem that good weather brings visitors out to a variety of attractions. The greatest increase that year, however, was in visits to gardens and garden centres which went up by a massive 12 per cent. Interest in gardens has continued to grow and those ranked highest in the UK are:

- Kew Gardens, London
- Stapeley Water Gardens, Cheshire
- Royal Botanical Gardens, Edinburgh
- Botanic Gardens, Glasgow
- Trentham Gardens, Stoke-on-Trent.

Itineraries

In order to work efficiently in a travel agency or tourist information centre, you need to be able to give information on what to see and how to get there, but it is equally important to be able to give a client some idea of how long it will take to reach a destination.

Maps and distance charts are used to estimate the miles or kilometres between places. The time taken to cover the distance then depends on the speed at which the person is travelling.

When calculating the times needed for a journey:

- first estimate the distance
- estimate the travel time by dividing the distance by the average speed
- suggest a break in the journey every 2 hours or every 100 miles, whichever is most convenient.

Distance charts can be found in atlases, guide books and even diaries.

Diagram 1.3 on page 6 shows a simple version of a distance chart which appears as a triangle.

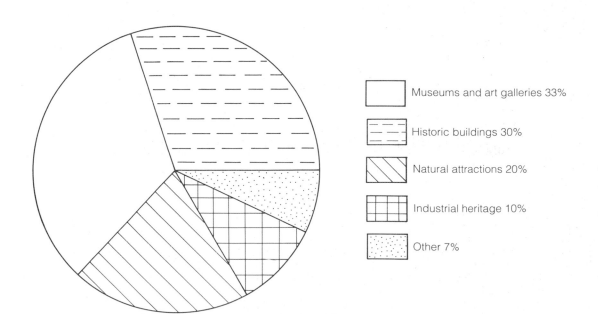

Museums and art galleries 33%

Historic buildings 30%

Natural attractions 20%

Industrial heritage 10%

Other 7%

Diagram 1.2   Pie chart showing the relative appeal of various types of attractions – based on over 5000 attractions monitored by the National Tourist Boards in 1990

Aberdeen	Aberdeen											
Birmingham	405	Birmingham										
Cambridge	446	100	Cambridge									
Dover	559	182	112	Dover								
Exeter	559	162	218	242	Exeter							
Glasgow	142	287	350	463	441	Glasgow						
Hull	341	124	123	236	279	245	Hull					
Leicester	412	39	68	169	191	299	87	Leicester				
Manchester	329	79	154	255	235	211	93	87	Manchester			
Oxford	466	64	80	129	138	350	156	69	142	Oxford		
Perth	81	329	371	484	484	61	265	322	254	390	Perth	
York	303	127	151	264	289	207	38	103	64	172	228	York
London	492	110	54	72	170	392	168	98	184	57	417	196	London

Diagram 1.3   Distance chart

To find the appropriate mileage:

♦ find the place you are leaving down the left hand side
♦ find the place you are going to along the slope
♦ once you have found both places, use your finger or a ruler to trace across the line from the left hand name until you are directly under the other name
♦ the number you have reached will give the mileage between the two places.

For example, if you wish to travel from Manchester to Hull, you locate Manchester down the left hand side and then move across reading the numbers 329, 79, 154, 255, 235, 211, until you reach 93 for Hull. The distance between Manchester and Hull is 93 miles.

Distance charts may be given in miles, kilometres or both. It is useful to remember that 8 kilometres are equal to 5 miles. You may be asked by a client to change kilometres into miles. To do this you multiply by $\frac{5}{8}$. So:

$$40 \text{ kilometres} = 40 \times \frac{5}{8} = \frac{200}{8} = 25 \text{ miles}$$

Similarly, to convert from miles to kilometres multiply by $\frac{8}{5}$. So:

$$25 \text{ miles} = 25 \times \frac{8}{5} = \frac{200}{5} = 40 \text{ kilometres}.$$

Sometimes you may have to give an indication of distance for smaller places which are not included in charts. To do this you will need to be able to gauge distances on a map. Diagram 1.4 shows a simple extract from a map. You will need an A4 sheet of paper and a pencil.

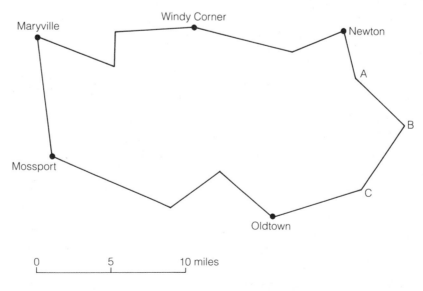

Diagram 1.4   A simple map

To estimate the distance between Newtown and Oldtown:

♦ place a corner of the A4 sheet of paper on the dot marking the centre of Newtown, making sure that a long edge lies on the road, until you reach point (A)

♦ now put the pencil point down firmly at this point on the paper and swing the edge of the paper around until it is once again lying along the road

♦ at point (B) you will again need to use the pencil as a pivot to swing the edge of the paper around onto the road

♦ continue in this way until you reach Oldtown and then mark the point reached on the edge of the paper

♦ now place the edge of the paper against the scale and read off the mileage. You will have to place it against the scale several times because the distance is greater than the ten miles given.

Using the edge of the paper in this way you have in fact just stretched out the road into a straight line.

Another way of measuring distances on maps is to use a piece of string and lay it along the route. If you start at Newtown and finish at Oldtown, when you take up the piece of string it will be the length of the road on the map. You can then read off the mileage by measuring the length of string against the scale in the same way as above. This is a simpler method than using paper and pencil but, whereas paper is usually available, balls of string are not so common!

Through the following activity you can familiarise yourself with some basic UK geographical facts.

◇ **Activity:** *Atlas reading* ◇

Copy the blank map of the UK and, with the help of an atlas, fill in the following information.

1 Draw in the borders between England, Wales, Scotland and Northern Ireland.

2 Mark and name the capitals London, Cardiff, Edinburgh and Belfast.

3 Make a collection of current ferry brochures and use them to mark and name UK ferry ports on the map.

4 With the aid of an AA manual, or any other suitable reference material, mark and name the motorways of England, Wales and Scotland.

5 Using an atlas or other suitable reference material, mark the following airports on your map: London (Heathrow, Gatwick, Stansted); Luton; Birmingham; Manchester; Leeds/ Bradford; Newcastle; Cardiff; Glasgow.

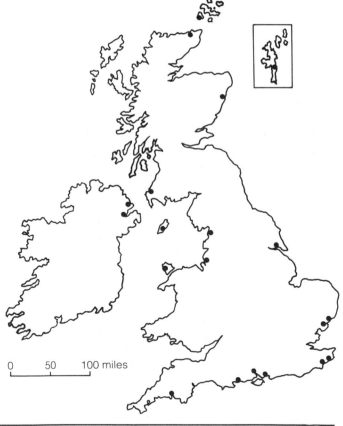

0   50   100 miles

2 Introduction to UK Travel Geography

This introductory chapter gives an overview of the wide variety of tourist attractions in the UK. These attractions include:

♦ **natural attractions**
♦ **historical buildings**
♦ **museums and art galleries**
♦ **industrial heritage**
♦ **theme parks**
♦ **leisure complexes.**

The chapters which follow will give detailed descriptions of the attractions in each of the specific areas of the country.

Main Tourist attractions in the UK

Natural attractions

The Countryside Commission was established in 1968 as an Advisory Body with responsibility for conservation of natural beauty in England and Wales and with a mandate to encourage facilities for recreation in the countryside. In 1967 the Countryside Commission for Scotland was set up but it merged with the Scottish National Heritage in 1991. The Countryside Commission has powers to designate:

♦ National Parks
♦ Areas of Outstanding Natural Beauty (AONB)
♦ Long Distance Paths or National Trails.

National Parks offer walks and drives through varied scenery and no one could forget a sight such as that in the North Yorkshire Moors in late summer when the ground is covered with a mass of purple heather.

A Ranger Service is available in the National Parks to guide visitors through easy or medium walks.

Diagram 2.1   The National Parks of England and Wales

For the more experienced walkers there are routes such as the Cleveland Way which circles the northern edges of the North Yorkshire Moors or the 40-mile Lyke Wake Walk which crosses the Moors from Osmotherley to Ravenscar.

Snowdonia National Park, in North Wales, covers over 800 square miles and is dominated by Snowdon itself which at 3569 feet (1085 m) is the highest mountain in Wales. The scenery in the Park offers a mixture of mountains, lakes and deep valleys and there are some noted beauty spots such as Betws-y-Coed.

The Countryside Commission has designated many places as Areas of Outstanding Natural Beauty (AONB.). These areas vary in size and include mountains, fells and dales, cliffs, sand dunes and tidal flats as well as woods and areas preserved for wildlife. Diagram 2.2 shows the AONB in England and Wales and the Heritage Coasts.

Heritage Coasts cover some 730 miles of coastline and preserve areas of particular beauty ranging from magnificent cliffs to flat sand dunes. Heritage Coasts are recommended by the Countryside Commission, but they are normally designated and protected by local authorities.

Most of the coast of the island of Anglesey is protected as an AONB for its unspoilt beaches and bird colonies. The Cotswolds, Britain's second largest AONB, is an area of limestone hill country with attractive Cotswold-stone towns and villages. Chichester Harbour with its sea creeks and tidal flats is a yachtsman's paradise. The Norfolk Coast, which is also preserved as a Heritage Coastline, is a unique area of sand dunes, shingle ridges, mud flats and saltings. A 60-mile stretch of the Kent Downs as well as extensive areas of Dorset and Hampshire include magnificent scenery as well as some attractive villages.

The Lochs and Highlands of Scotland have scenery and beauty which it would be hard to match in any part of the world. Diagram 2.3 shows the designated AONB and Forest Parks in Scotland.

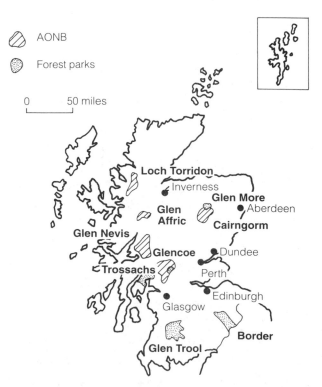

Diagram 2.2   Areas of Outstanding Natural Beauty (AONB) and Heritage Coasts in England and Wales

Diagram 2.3   Areas of Outstanding Natural Beauty (AONB) and Forest Parks in Scotland

Long distance paths and bridleways, or National Trails, are designated by the Countryside Commission so that it is possible to enjoy these areas, avoiding major towns and roads as far as possible .

Diagram 2.4   National Trails in England and Wales

Diagram 2.4 shows nine of the routes for National Trails approved by the Secretary of State for the Environment or for Wales.

- ◆ The Pennine Way was the first long distance footpath to be designated and it links three National Parks and stretches from Derbyshire to the Scottish border. It can be walked in 14 days, or even less by the exceptionally fit.
- ◆ The longest footpath is the South West Peninsula Coast Path which follows the old coastguards' paths through North Devon, Cornwall, South Devon and Dorset.
- ◆ The South Downs Way is the only long distance bridleway, which means that horse-riders and cyclists as well as walkers can enjoy the path following the ridge of the South Downs in an AONB which stretches from Eastbourne to South Harting, near Petersfield.

The National Trust is the country's largest private landowner. Its properties include farms, woodland, nature reserves, 50 villages and hamlets and many stretches of coastline. The Trust has a special campaign called Enterprise Neptune devoted to acquiring and preserving coastline property, and currently it protects 500 miles of coastline in England, Wales and Northern Ireland. There is an independent National Trust for Scotland. With concern for conservation, the National Trust controls access to its land and makes every effort to screen car parks and service buildings from view.

The increasing importance of leisure time and popularity of water sports accounts for the rise in bookings for canal holidays in the 1980s. Diagram 2.5 shows the network of canals and waterways throughout England and Wales. It is possible to hire barges and boats in most parts of the country and travel at a leisurely pace along these networks.

Diagram 2.5   Canals and waterways in England and Wales

The Wildfowl and Wetlands Trust which was founded in 1946 by the late Sir Peter Scott provides eight centres around the country, six of them with collections of thousands of exotic wildfowl from all over the world. Special promotions are organised throughout the year to attract visitors to the centres. Diagram 2.6 shows the location of the centres in England, Scotland and Northern Ireland.

Diagram 2.6   Wildfowl and Wetland Centres in the UK

The most popular outdoor activities in the UK include:

- walking
- fishing
- horse riding
- climbing
- bird-watching

- cycling
- camping
- sailing
- potholing
- air sports.

Historical buildings

Historical buildings such as cathedrals, abbeys and castles hold a special fascination, especially for overseas visitors who want to capture the spirit of our culture. The Department of the Environment under the banner of English Heritage operates many of these properties. Fountains Abbey in Yorkshire, for instance, is said to be one of the finest examples in Europe of a

medieval monastery. Much of it is now in ruins, but it is still possible to trace the life of the monastic community who lived there.

Many British cities have magnificent cathedrals, such as York, Winchester, Salisbury and the post-war cathedral at Coventry.

In Wales there are castles dating from the earliest times to the series of castles built or strengthened by Edward I in the thirteenth and fourteenth century. Caernarfon Castle was the scene for the investiture of the Prince of Wales and is one of Britain's best known historical sites. Chepstow Castle, which stands above the Wye river, was probably the first stone castle in Britain. It was added to right up to the Civil War and so illustrates different periods of castle building.

Britain is rich in country houses which are not only furnished in the style of their period but have been lived in by the same family for generations. Indeed, in some of the smaller properties it is possible to chat with the owners. Privately owned homes sometimes specialise in features which are of interest to their owner. One such is Arley Hall in Cheshire which has spectacular gardens and also encourages local craftspeople to demonstrate their skills to visitors.

Even the Queen opens her doors to the public at Sandringham in the summer. There are extensive car parks outside the main gate, and the grounds, gardens and main house can all be visited.

The National Trust cares for a wide variety of buildings of architectural and historical interest. These range from humble cottages which may have been rented to tenants, to larger houses of country families.

- The home of the Browne family at Townend, Troutbeck in the Lake District dates from the seventeenth century and contains much of the family's personal furniture and belongings.
- Sizergh Castle in Cumbria was in the Strickland family from the thirteenth century until it was handed into the care of the National Trust in 1950.
- Little Moreton Hall in Cheshire is a fine example of a traditional timber-frame black and white construction.

The National Trust manages 140 country houses, some of which, like Hardwick Hall in Derbyshire, Petworth House in West Sussex and Blickling Hall in Norfolk have important collections of art and furniture. The gardens of many of these houses are also of interest. The guide book of Blickling Hall takes the visitor through the gardens giving full details of shrubs and trees.

The most popular UK historical properties are:

♦ Tower of London
♦ Edinburgh Castle
♦ Roman Baths and Pump Room, Bath
♦ Windsor Castle, State Apartments
♦ Stonehenge, Wiltshire.

Museums and art galleries

Throughout the country we have a wide network of museums and art galleries, many of which are free to the public. From the British Museum, with its worldwide reputation, to small local collections, most museums have changed their image in recent years and now present a less formal and more welcoming environment for children.

In the Liverpool Museum, children queue to be the first into the natural history section during afternoons in the school holidays when there are countless activities and exhibits for them to use. The Science Museum in Kensington could keep anyone, child or adult, occupied for days. On the five floors of the museum visitors can explore space, engineering, chemistry, oceanography and medicine.

Several museums have introduced drama to help interpret their collections. The National Museum of Photography at Bradford has a team of dancers who interpret both recent photographic history and modern photographic collections in a unique art form. The Museum of the Moving Image on the South Bank of the Thames in London uses actors both to interpret their displays for visitors and to act as security staff in all areas of the museum.

Not surprisingly, the five most visited UK museums and art galleries are all based in London:

♦ British Museum
♦ National Gallery
♦ Natural History Museum
♦ Tate Gallery
♦ Science Museum.

Industrial heritage

In recent years industrial heritage has become a popular subject for tourism. Buildings dating from the industrial revolution have been restored and tools and implements associated with local trades are displayed in an attractive and informative manner. At the Wrekin Heritage Site in Shropshire it is possible, within a 10-mile radius, to visit the Aerospace Museum at RAF Cosford, the Ironbridge Gorge Museum and the Midland Motor Museum as well as the Severn Valley Railway. Ironbridge, which claims to be the birthplace of the Industrial Revolution, has a total of six museum sites for the visitor. Open air living museums of industrial heritage have been developed at:

♦ Beamish Open Air Museum, Co. Durham
♦ The Black Country Museum, Dudley
♦ Blists Hill, Ironbridge
♦ Morwellham Quay, Devon
♦ Weald and Downland Museum, near Chichester.

In these open air museums interpreters are dressed in period costume to enhance the experience of the past for visitors. Artefacts and period buildings are used at Beamish to recreate 1913. Visitors can stroll through the local Co-op, can visit the dentist where instruments and smells recall the past vividly for older guests, or can even go down the confined passages of a drift mine, escorted by retired miners in period dress who bring the working conditions of the past to life.

Beamish Open Air Museum, Co. Durham

Theme parks

Theme parks hold great attraction for all ages in all parts of the country. These parks usually have fairground rides for children, teenagers and adults. Many have beautiful gardens, and all aim to provide enough undercover entertainment to keep guests happy for at least one full day.

- Alton Towers in Staffordshire is very centrally located for tourists from most parts of England and Wales and its popularity testifies to this. It not only contains a fairground to rival any other for youngsters, but its gardens are also a pleasure for more sedate visitors.
- Thorpe Park in Surrey is accessible to tourists in the Greater London area and each summer has over a million visitors. The organisers claim that there are up to 4 hours of entertainment completely under cover, should the weather be bad.
- The American Adventure in Derbyshire and the Magical Kingdom of Camelot in Lancashire, whilst not on the same scale as the other parks, nevertheless offer great days out, with undercover entertainment and thrilling and daring rides.
- Granada Studios in Manchester is a new style of theme park which takes the visitor into the magical world of television where everything is not what it seems. Guests can walk down famous streets, drink in famous bars, become a child in a giant's world or chat with the housekeeper of Sherlock Holmes in his private study. Modern rides such as Motion Master and a selection of live shows make this a full day trip for most visitors.

These theme parks also have an eye to the business world with each one offering conference and business hospitality facilities.

Leisure Complexes

Leisure and sports facilities are becoming very popular with today's emphasis on fitness and health. Some local authorities have opened their own facilities, such as the dry ski slope at Southampton and the Waves Water Fun Centre at Blackburn. Holiday centres provide leisure facilities and entertainment with either half-board or self-catering accommodation.

- Center Parcs in Nottinghamshire and East Anglia are among the largest privately owned complexes. Each centre has a central dome over the swimming area, creating a subtropical paradise. Accommodation is in modern purpose-built cabins and on-site facilities include cycling, walking, adventure trails and evening entertainment.
- Butlin's holiday camps were totally updated during the 1980s. Five of the original camps have been renamed Holiday Worlds and the brochure also offers holidays in five hotels. The Holiday Worlds offer self-catering, half- or full-board accommodation. Entertainment facilities include fairgrounds, fully equipped theatres, sub-tropical water worlds, and clubs to occupy children of all ages.

A Butlin's sub-tropical water world

- Fred Pontin started his holiday camps in the late 1940s and today's brochure offers a choice of 20 Holiday Centres around Britain, as well as Plêmont Bay on Jersey. Five of the mainland Centres are Chalet Hotels with full table service as well as all the entertainment offered in the other centres. Five of Pontins holiday centres offer holidays for adults only. These are very popular with older people, particularly during the summer months of the school holidays.

These leisure and holiday centres offer holidays which are very often enjoyed by three generations of a family. Some of the centres which have been built on flat land near to the sea are also particularly suitable for holidays for the disabled.

The management in most larger hotels throughout the country realise the attraction of these complexes and it is not uncommon to find a hotel offering not just a small swimming pool but also a jacuzzi, sauna and sunbeds together with a mini gym. Such facilities are enjoyable for visitors and add to the potential of the hotel for staging conferences and business hospitality.

The following activity should help you to increase your awareness of the variety of UK tourist attractions.

◇ **Activity:** *Sources of information* ◇

Add your own suggestions to the following lists.

Tourists like to go to

The seaside
Blackpool, Brighton, …

Beautiful countryside
The Scottish Highlands, Snowdonia, …

Museums and art galleries
The Tate Gallery, Manchester Museum of Science and Industry, …

Cathedrals, Abbeys and Castles
Salisbury, Conwy Castle, Rievaulx Abbey, …

Stately homes
Longleat, Blickling Hall, …

Theme parks
Alton Towers, Thorpe Park, …

Leisure complexes
Center Parcs, Ski-Rossendale, …

Shopping malls
Covent Garden, MetroCentre, Albert Dock, …

Specialist tourist attractions
Madame Tussaud's, Granada Studios, …

Industrial heritage and folk attractions
Ironbridge, Wigan Pier, …

Your lists can be as long as you wish and you can, of course, add your own headings.

---

3 London

Tourists can have countless reasons for visiting London:

- **a family day out**
- **shopping**
- **visits to museums or art galleries**
- **a business meeting with some sightseeing**
- **foreign visitors wanting to see royalty**
- **a night out at the theatre**
- **a show at Earl's Court.**

London is accessible from any part of Britain because most motorways converge on the capital and the M25 gives access around London. Rail links also converge on London stations, and the airports of Heathrow and Gatwick bring a constant flow of foreign visitors.

London Transport issues a range of free leaflets about travel on the underground and buses. You should contact London Transport for a selection of maps so that you can locate all the places mentioned. You will need a London bus and underground map to do the activity on page 18. London Transport also offers a variety of Travelcards and Networkcards which enable tourists to have cheaper and more convenient travel during their stay in the capital. A card which is valid on the underground and the buses works out much cheaper than paying for each individual journey and cuts out the need to queue at stations.

We shall study the attractions of London under the headings of

- famous landmarks, such as Westminster Abbey and the Tower of London
- famous streets, such as Oxford Street and Piccadilly Circus
- royal London, with its palaces and gardens

- the River Thames, from Westminster to Greenwich, and the attractions on its banks
- markets and shopping areas
- museums, art galleries and theatres
- modern attractions, such as Madame Tussaud's and the London Dungeon.

Famous landmarks

Starting in the West End and moving down-river we will consider some of the better known landmarks of London. Many of these are familiar to people from all over the country, mainly because of television news coverage.

The Royal Albert Hall, in Kensington, is an immense domed circular hall, built in 1871 in honour of the Prince Consort. It is famous as the home of the Proms during July, August and September and the Remembrance Day Commemoration in November.

In Westminster are the Palace of Westminster and Westminster Abbey. The Palace of Westminster is better known as the Houses of Parliament and the Victoria Clock Tower at the south end is affectionately called Big Ben. By contacting their Member of Parliament, British tourists can arrange to have a tour of the Houses of Parliament. There is no charge for the tour but it is usual to give something to the guide. Westminster Abbey has been the site of royal coronations and weddings since 1065 and it is also the burial place of monarchs, poets, and statesmen. The Abbey is still the centre of a praying community but visitors are welcome to take a tour of the tombs and memorial statues.

In the City of London are St Paul's Cathedral, the Bank of England, the Tower of London and Tower Bridge. St Paul's, Christopher Wren's magnificent domed cathedral, still retains its majesty when viewed from the Thames in spite of surrounding office blocks. The dome has three galleries, the most famous of which is the Whispering Gallery. The Bank of England is a massive, windowless stone structure in Threadneedle Street in the City. An adjoining museum gives visitors information about day-to-day life in the Bank. The Tower of London has been a royal residence, a prison and a place of execution. It draws tourists in their thousands to see the Yeomen of the Guard and the Crown Jewels within its walls. Tower Bridge is possibly one of the most familiar sights to foreign tourists. A pedestrian walkway exists between the twin towers and it is possible to view the machinery used to raise the bridge to allow ships to enter the Pool of London.

Famous streets

Many London streets are famous for their shops but these we shall consider later. Whitehall, which runs between Westminster Bridge and Trafalgar Square is well known to millions because 10 Downing Street, the residence of the Prime Minster, is just off Whitehall. Scotland Yard and the Cenotaph are in Whitehall and Horse Guards Parade, the barracks of the Queen's Guard, is to the side of Whitehall.

Trafalgar Square is famous for its flock of pigeons and as a rallying point for demonstrations of all kinds. In the centre is Nelson's Column, flanked by lions and fountains, and to the north side of the square is the National Gallery.

Leading out of Trafalgar Square, parallel with the River Thames, is the Strand. Between the River and the Strand lie two of London's four Inns of Court, the Inner and Middle. This is a peaceful enclave of mostly seventeenth-century courts and alleyways. To the north of the Strand, towards Piccadilly Circus and Leicester Square, is theatreland, with theatres too numerous to list. Further north again between Shaftesbury Avenue and Oxford Street is Soho, famous for its restaurants and notorious for its stripshows.

Royal London

Buckingham Palace, the principal home of the Queen, draws tourists all day to the end of The Mall. The palace is not open to the public, although it is possible to visit the Royal Mews and the Queen's Gallery. Public notices are pinned to the gate so a crowd will always gather when there is any royal news. The Changing of the Guard takes place each day at 11.30 a.m. with a band leading the new guard to the palace and the old one back to its barracks.

Hampton Court Palace at Kingston-upon-Thames was one of Henry VIII's favourite residences. Nowadays it is open to the public and with its Great Hall, Tudor and seventeenth-century

Hampton Court Palace, London

staterooms, reconstructed kitchens, maze and riverside gardens, the estate affords plenty of interest for a full day out.

London is also rich in Royal Parks which are accessible to the public. The Royal Parks include Hyde Park, Green Park, Kensington Gardens, Regent's Park, St James's Park and Richmond Park. Hyde Park is probably the most famous with the Serpentine Lake, Speakers' Corner at the corner of the park nearest to Marble Arch, and the pathway, still used for riders, called Rotten Row, which is a corruption of *Route du Roi*, meaning the King's Way.

The River Thames

A cruise down the Thames can give newcomers to London a different perspective on the attractions. Cruises start from Westminster Pier in the shadow of the Houses of Parliament and the statue of Boadicea. Passing under Hungerford Bridge, a popular foot-crossing from Waterloo to Charing Cross Station, on your left is Cleopatra's Needle, a 3000-year-old Egyptian obelisk, and on your right is the South Bank Complex. This complex includes the Festival Hall, the National Theatre and the National Film Theatre with its Museum of the Moving Image.

Having passed Southwark, HMS *Belfast*, a World War II cruiser comes into sight. This cruiser was the largest and most powerful ever built for the Royal Navy and it is now permanently moored as a museum. Tower Bridge lies behind HMS *Belfast* and the Tower of London is on the left.

Next to the Tower of London is St Katherine's Dock, where the buildings have been renovated to house offices and craft shops; the dock itself is now a marina. The Thames flows on past Wapping and the Isle of Dogs, where modern accommodation has transformed much of the East End.

Finally, the cruise reaches Greenwich with Wren's superb Royal Naval College, the Old Royal Observatory with the brass Greenwich Mean Line on the ground and, moored near the pier, are the two historic ships the *Cutty Sark* and *Gypsy Moth IV*.

Markets and shopping areas

Shopping is very much a tourist activity, especially in London. The two most famous markets are Petticoat Lane and Portobello Road. Petticoat Lane Market on Sunday mornings actually takes place in Middlesex Street in the East End of London and it has all the charm and flavour of real cockney London. Portobello Road is in Notting Hill, north of Kensington. This market takes place throughout the week and has a very West Indian flavour. On Saturdays, the usual stalls are joined by specialist antique dealers, buskers and entertainers.

Harrods is probably the best known of the London shops. The Knightsbridge store justifies this appeal, not only with its extraordinary prices but with the equally extraordinary decor of some of the departments within the store. Oxford Street and Regent Street are always busy, but especially so at Christmas time. Within these streets can be found every sort of shop and at least one branch of most chain stores. Bond Street is well known for its jewellers, art dealers and expensive boutiques.

Museums, art galleries and theatres

The London museums are too numerous to list but the more important ones are the British Museum in Great Russell Street, not far from Euston Station, which contains a wealth of treasures from all over the world, and the Science Museum, the Geological Museum, the Natural History Museum and the Victoria and Albert Museum, all of which can be found in the area immediately behind the Royal Albert Hall, in Kensington.

The more important art galleries are the National Gallery in Trafalgar Square and the nearby National Portrait Gallery. Both galleries have paintings of worldwide importance. The Tate Gallery, on the banks of the Thames, up-river from Westminster, specialises in modern paintings.

Theatres are mainly in the West End, the area between the Strand and Shaftesbury Avenue.

Current programmes are listed in the London newspapers and late bookings can be made for shows in a booth in Leicester Square, although buyers should beware of getting tickets for seats behind pillars or right under the stage! Ticket touts try to sell seats to tourists for the more popular shows, which are booked up months in advance, but generally speaking these touts do not have the better seats for sale.

The Barbican in the City of London is an ambitious scheme to recreate a living community in the City. Tower blocks of flats overlook the complex which contains the Museum of London, exhibition halls, a concert hall and a theatre which is the London home to the Royal Shakespeare Company.

◇ **Activity:** *Day excursion on public transport* ◇

To do this activity you will need a London Transport map and a guide to Central London which shows the underground and key bus routes.

The underground lines are shown in colours as indicated in the key at the bottom of the map. The bus numbers are shown in circles at the main route junctions. To travel from one place to another you must be certain that the number of bus you choose to use is shown in the appropriate circles at the beginning and end of your journey.

Your task is to plan a day excursion in London for yourself.

Select six places or landmarks which you would like to see in a day. Your trip will start at 9.30 a.m. and assume you have a Travelcard for the day. Before you start, decide what time your day will end.

Arrange your six places in order for visiting. Using the Central London map choose routes between your selected places and try to estimate the travelling time. Remember that buses travel slowly during the rush hour in the early evening. Draw up and complete a chart similar to the one which follows.

Day excursion in London				
From	Time	bus/ underground	To	Sights to be seen
Gloucester Road	9.30	Piccadilly line	Knightsbridge	Harrods, window shopping
Brompton Road	10.30	73 bus	Oxford Street	Marble Arch, shopping
Oxford Street	11.30	1 bus	Trafalgar Square	Nelson's Column, National Gallery

Modern attractions in London

Wembley Stadium is known to millions through television and visitors can have a guided tour of the complex. The main events taking place each year are:

April	Football League Cup Final
May	Rugby League Cup Final
	FA Cup Final.

Earl's Court is another well known venue and its shows and exhibitions draw many visitors to London. The main annual events are:

January	International Boat Show
March	Ideal Home Exhibition
July	Royal Tournament
November	World Travel Market
December	Smithfield Show

Madame Tussaud's has been a top attraction in London for many years. Next door, the London Planetarium is also very popular and reduced priced tickets can be purchased for both attractions. The Rock Circus, offered by the same group, in Piccadilly Circus is an unusual combination of sound effects, waxworks and modern use of hydraulics and illusion. Also in Piccadilly Circus is the popular Guiness World of Records Exhibition bringing spectacular feats and records to life.

On the South Bank is the London Dungeon, claimed to be the only medieval horror museum in the world. Its realistic recreation of scenes of medieval torture is certainly not for the fainthearted! At Tower Hill Pageant which opened opposite the Tower of London in 1991, visitors are transported in automated vehicles through the 2000 years of London's Thameside history.

◇ Summary of London attractions ◇

Famous landmarks

Royal Albert Hall, Kensington
Palace of Westminster, Houses of Parliament
Westminster Abbey
St Paul's Cathedral, City of London
Tower of London
Tower Bridge
Bank of England, Threadneedle Street,
    City of London

Famous streets

Whitehall
Trafalgar Square
Downing Street
Strand
Piccadilly Circus
Leicester Square
Shaftesbury Avenue
Oxford Street

Royal London

Buckingham Palace, The Mall
Hampton Court Palace, Kingston-upon-
    Thames
Royal parks:
    Hyde Park
    Kensington Gardens
    Richmond Park
    Green Park
    Regent's Park
    St James's Park

The River Thames

Westminster Pier
Cleopatra's Needle
South Bank Complex
HMS *Belfast*
Tower Bridge
Tower of London
St Katherine's Dock
Isle of Dogs
Greenwich

Markets and shopping areas

Petticoat Lane Market, Middlesex Street
Portobello Road Market, Notting Hill
Harrods, Brompton Road
Oxford Street
Regent Street
Bond Street

Museums, art galleries and theatres

British Museum, Great Russell Street
Science Museum, Kensington
Geological Museum, Kensington
Natural History Museum, Kensington
Victoria and Albert Museum, Kensington
National Gallery, Trafalgar Square
National Portrait Gallery, Trafalgar Square
Tate Gallery
West End theatres
Barbican, City of London (Royal Shakespeare
    Company)
Museum of London
Museum of the Moving Image, South Bank

Modern attractions

Wembley Stadium
Earl's Court
Madame Tussaud's
London Planetarium
Rock Circus
Guiness World of Records
London Dungeon
Tower Hill Pageant

London festivals and ceremonies

March	Harness Horse Parade, Regent's Park
	Oxford and Cambridge Boat Race, Putney to Mortlake
April	London Marathon
May	Chelsea Flower Show
June	Trooping the Colour, Horse Guards Parade, Whitehall
	Lawn Tennis Championships, Wimbledon
August	Notting Hill Carnival
October	State Opening of Parliament, Westminster
November	RAC London to Brighton Veteran Car Run, Hyde Park
	Lord Mayor's Show, City of London
	Remembrance Day Service, The Cenotaph, Whitehall
December	Christmas Tree, Trafalgar Square
	Illuminated Decorations, Regent St and Oxford St

4 Southern England

In this section we will consider the area covered by the Southern and the South East English Tourist Boards. This area covers the counties of:

- **Dorset**
- **Hampshire**
- **Wiltshire (South)**
- **Surrey**
- **Kent**
- **West Sussex**
- **East Sussex**
- **the Isle of Wight.**

Access to this area is very easy from London from where the M3, M23, M20 and M2 radiate. Access from the west is by means of the M4 and access from the north is around London using the M25 to link with the required motorway moving south. Rail links to London are good through Network Southeast. There are links all along the coast and, through Salisbury, there are links to Bristol and Birmingham. Gatwick and Heathrow airports are in the area as well as Bournemouth airport and Southampton's Eastleigh airport, both of which have services to Scotland, the Channel Islands and the Continent. There are cross-channel ports right along the coast from Ramsgate to Weymouth making access easy for tourists from The Netherlands, Belgium and France.

Southampton is one of the foremost ports in Britain and is the home of the *QE2*. The maritime museum, archaelogical museum and several medieval restored houses make Southampton an interesting city for tourists. Portsmouth has strong links with Britain's naval role and markets itself as the 'Flagship of Maritime England'. Naval Heritage at Portsmouth includes:

- the Royal Naval Museum

- the *Mary Rose*, Henry VIII's warship which was raised from the seabed where it had lain since 1545
- the HMS *Victory*, Nelson's flagship
- HMS *Warrior*, the first ironclad warship dating from 1860, and
- the D–Day Museum, next to Southsea Castle, which is a permanent record of history's biggest sea-borne invasion in 1944.

The Southern Tourist Board examined its strategy for tourism as it entered the 1990s and concluded that business tourism, short breaks, day trips and general leisure activity were all on the increase. The implications for tourism were that whilst the traditional seaside market, which underpins much of the area's tourist industry, had to be maintained, new attractions would have to be developed. In line with this thinking, we will consider the attractions of Southern England under three sections:

- natural attractions of an area rich in beautiful countryside and coastline
- traditional seaside resorts from Margate to Bournemouth, with their miles of sand and 'bucket and spade' image

◆ modern attractions, many of which, such as the Canterbury Tales, are in fact in places which have traditionally drawn tourists.

Natural Attractions

The fact that much of Dorset, Hampshire, Sussex and Kent has been designated as Areas of Outstanding Natural Beauty (AONB) testifies to the beauty of the countryside in Southern England. The area between Winchester and the Sussex border is a pleasant rolling hill country with a mixture of woodlands and farmlands. South Hampshire has the attractive Solent coast from Hurst Castle to Calshot Castle, as well as the Beaulieu River. The Sussex Downs are rolling chalk hills extending from East Hampshire, across West Sussex and terminating at the Seven Sisters and Beachy Head in East Sussex. The Kent Downs is a 60-mile stretch of beautiful countryside which includes the North Downs Way, a recognised long distance footpath.

Coastal beauty is to be found in the Dorset AONB from the Isle of Purbeck to the Devon boundary. Chichester Harbour in West Sussex is an area of sea creeks and tidal flats, and 10 miles away the Wildfowl Trust's centre is set against the backdrop of Arundel Castle.

Between Southampton and Bournemouth lie 90 000 acres of the New Forest, a uniquely special area since the days of William the Conqueror. The famous ponies roam free through the area and visitors can occasionally glimpse royal red deer in the heart of the forest. There is a New Forest Museum and Visitor Centre at Lyndhurst, but visitors can best experience the Forest by walking through the woodlands, heath and glades.

Traditional Seaside Resorts

◆ Margate is the largest seaside resort in Kent and one of the oldest in the country. It was here that a Quaker named Benjamin Beale invented the Victorian bathing-machine so that ladies could get into the water without being watched by prying eyes. Nowadays Margate offers all the usual fun of the beach and the fair and the Bembom Brothers White Knuckle Theme Park.

East Sussex is rich in seaside resorts, the largest of which are Hastings, Eastbourne and Brighton.

◆ Hastings is a restrained resort which appeals to families, in spite of having a shingly rather than a sandy beach. Surprisingly, it is not the site of the famous battle of 1066, which actually took place six miles inland at a place which is appropriately called Battle. Battle Abbey, now a girls' school, has the field on which the battle took place within its grounds. The field still has an eerie atmosphere about it, even though it is only yards from a bustling town centre.

◆ Eastbourne claims to be one of the sunniest resorts in Britain and its elegance owes much to the Victorian planners who laid out the parks and gardens and built the pier. The Museum of the Royal National Lifeboat Institution is housed in the Wish Tower. There is also a Coastal Defence Museum housed in one of the Martello towers built in the 1800s to fend off invasion by Napoleon.

◆ Brighton owes its existence as a seaside resort to the Prince Regent, later George IV. His Royal Pavilion, built in an exotic Indian style, caused fashionable London to flock to the town in the eighteenth century. Elegant squares and terraces were built to accommodate the new visitors and it is not surprising that, with the advent of the railways in the 1850s, Brighton became one of the first seaside resorts to prosper. Nowadays it is a popular conference venue and the vast marina has moorings for over 2000 craft.

In Dorset, the neighbouring resorts of Bournemouth and Poole have retained their appeal over the years.

◆ Bournemouth has 7 miles of sandy beach which is kept clean enough to be awarded the 'Three Spades' of the Marine Conservation Society. The town is perched on 6 miles of clifftop giving stunning views from the numerous hotels and guesthouses. Bournemouth is a pretty resort with its shopping arcades, hanging flower baskets, bands in the park and many antique shops. Even Sotheby's has a branch in Bournemouth. Professional entertainment in a variety of theatres and halls ranges from traditional seaside comic shows to the Spectacular on Ice.

♦ Poole, only 5 miles away, is famous for its associations with sailing. Poole Harbour is said to be the largest natural harbour in the world, since much of Sydney's has been reclaimed. The resort has three small museums; Knoll Gardens and the Compton Acres Gardens; garden centres such as the Courtyard Centre, which offer traditional Dorset cream teas; and up-to-date modern attractions in the spectacular IceTrax, with three-quarters of an acre of ice ramps, ice trails and disco lighting, Splashdown water flumes and rides and the unique Tank Museum, one of the most comprehensive collections of armoured fighting vehicles. The local Swanage Steam Railway offers trips through the surrounding beauty of the Purbeck Hills.

◇ **Activity:** *Day trip by coach* ◇

Your college has strong links with a college in the north of England which also offers travel and tourism courses. You have been asked to organise a day trip for 30 17-year-old students from the college who will be attending the World Travel Market in London in November. They intend to stay two nights in London and would like a coach trip to give them 'a taste of the South'.

The day trip should include:

♦ typical scenery of the area
♦ a stately home
♦ a good shopping area
♦ a coastal resort or town
♦ other attractions you think would appeal.

For the purpose of this activity you are not concerned with costs but you should prepare a detailed itinerary of suggestions for the college. You have two weeks to complete this project.

Modern attractions

Lord Montague was one of the first to realise the potential of modern attractions when he opened his collection of veteran cars to the public in 1952. Beaulieu, on the edge of the New Forest, is now one of the major attractions in Britain. Visitors can see the National Motor Museum; take an exciting ride through the history of motoring; travel around the grounds on a monorail; visit an exhibition about the original abbey and monastic life, before the dissolution of the monasteries; and meet actors who help to bring Victorian times to life again in Palace House.

Where else in the world could you visit the Turin Shroud, the Chinese Terracotta Warriors and the tomb of Tutankhamun all in a week's holiday? All of these are subjects of new exhibitions in Southern England.

♦ The Turin Shroud Exhibition explores the mystery of the Shroud looking at the latest evidence in Bournemouth.
♦ Also in Bournemouth, Qin Shi Huangdi and his terracotta warriors have been magnificently recreated in life-size models.
♦ Thirty miles away at Dorchester is the only Tutankhamun exhibition outside Egypt. The tomb and treasures have been recreated using sight, sound and smells.

The technique of using sights, sounds and smells was first exploited in the Jorvik Viking Centre, in York. Heritage Projects grew out of that experience and the company has produced three very unusual attractions in Southern England.

♦ A Day at the Wells, in Kent, recreates eighteenth-century Tunbridge Wells which was a scandalous place to stay in Georgian England.
♦ The White Cliffs Experience Historium lets visitors row a real Roman galley, clamber the rigging of an old Dover ferry and pick their way through the glowing embers of the 1944 Dover streets as the wail of the air raid siren dies away.
♦ The Canterbury Tales lets the visitor step back to medieval times to become one of Chaucer's band of pilgrims walking from Southwark to Canterbury. Along the way five of the well known pilgrims recount their tales of romance, chivalry, jealousy, pride and avarice.

Winchester in Hampshire markets modern-day attractions in the Crusades Experience, Marwell Zoo and nearby Broadlands.

♦ The Crusades Experience, within the walls and precincts of St John's House, takes visitors back to the time of King Richard the Lionheart and the Third Crusade. Crusaders, monks and various twelfth-century figures bring the colour and violence of the period to life.

♦ Marwell Zoo has a wildlife conservation and breeding area, train rides through the park, a farmyard and play areas as well as the usual big cats, zebras and monkeys one expects to find in a large zoo.

♦ Broadlands, the former home of Lord Mountbatten and famous for royal honeymoons, has installed a modern multi-screen audiovisual presentation about the life of Lord Mountbatten.

Theme Parks are very popular with families and teenagers and Southern England has its share of these too. Hampshire has Paultons and the Pyramids and Surrey has Thorpe Park and Chessington World of Adventures.

♦ Paultons Park near Romsey has entertainment aimed at families with young children. Set in parkland and gardens it has fun activities, birds, animals and a miniature railway.

♦ The Pyramids at Southsea is a leisure complex with slides, wave machine, surf, and a video wall showing cartoons, all in a tropical atmosphere.

♦ Thorpe Park is a landscaped theme park created on the site of an old gravel pit. The rides and attractions are on an island around which visitors can travel by boat or minitrain. The park is designed so that visitors can have up to 4 hours of entertainment completely undercover should the weather be bad.

♦ Chessington World of Adventures was formerly a traditional zoo but has been modernised in recent years by the Madame Tussaud's Group. The theme park now includes fairground rides, a safari skyway, and Professor Burps Bubbleworks – a musical fantasy ride.

Many other modern attractions have been created in Southern England but the above give a flavour of the variety and technology being used to attract day visitors, and those on short breaks as well as those looking for a traditional holiday week by the sea.

Isle of Wight

The 147 square miles of the Isle of Wight attract over a million visitors each year. The island has an abundance of attractions and beaches, and over 40 per cent of the island is designated as AONB. The County Structure Plan recognises the importance of tourism to the local economy with support and encouragement for all aspects of tourism. In particular the council encourages development of Conference Centres, all-weather facilities and improved standards of accommodation.

Car ferries connect the island with Portsmouth, Southampton and Lymington with crossing times from 30 minutes to an hour. The hovercraft for foot-passengers from Southsea to Ryde takes only eight minutes. The main airport on the island is at Sandown and road/rail Rover tickets give visitors access to the public transport system for a day, a week or four weeks. These Rover cards also entitle visitors to a 75 per cent reduction on coach tours and discounted entrance to several visitor attractions.

Activities on the island include:

♦ walking
♦ cycling
♦ hang-gliding
♦ fishing
♦ golf
♦ sailing

The Depth Charge at Thorpe Park, Surrey

- windsurfing
- mountain biking
- jet-skiing
- water sports
- bowling
- sports centres.

As well as enjoying the natural beauty and coastlines, nature lovers can visit a variety of animal parks including the zoo at Sandown, bird parks at St Lawrence and Seaview, a farm park at Yafford and a donkey sanctuary at Newport. Historical interest on the island ranges from Roman remains to sites visited by famous poets and politicians and several stately homes including Osborne House, the former home of Queen Victoria. Additional interest is provided at Arreton Manor with a Wireless Museum and at Haseley Manor with demonstrations of sweet-making and pottery. The Isle of Wight is sometimes referred to as 'England in miniature' with its olde-worlde villages of thatched roofs, traditional pubs and cream teas.

- Cowes, on the north of the island, is home to the international yachting regatta during the first week in August, and also has pleasant pedestrianised shopping areas. West Cowes is favoured by the yachting community and East Cowes has Osborne House, the former royal residence.
- Newport is the island's commercial and administrative centre and attracts visitors to its Tuesday market, the remains of a Roman villa and the pirate ship moored on the quayside. Nearby Robin Hill Adventure Park is a paradise of slides, boating, assault courses and crazy golf.

- Bembridge and Ryde on the east coast both have small attractive harbours and traditional seaside shops, cinemas and theatres. Brading, near Bembridge, has a wax museum set in an ancient rectory mansion, a toy museum and a Roman villa with preserved mosaics.
- The other east coast resorts of Sandown, Shanklin and Ventnor offer traditional family entertainment. The Blackgang Chine Fantasy Park near to Ventnor has a variety of amusements set in themed areas in a cliff top garden. Godshill, to the west of Shanklin, offers cream teas in a village setting as well as a model village which is illuminated on summer evenings.
- On the western tip of the island are the multi-coloured sand cliffs of the Needles. The Needles Pleasure Park offers boat trips to the famous lighthouse, a chairlift to the beach and a variety of amusements and small shops.

Diagram 4.1   Summary map of Southern England

◇ Summary of attractions ◇

Seaside resorts

Margate, Kent
Hastings, East Sussex
Eastbourne, East Sussex
Brighton, East Sussex
Bournemouth, Dorset
Poole, Dorset
Sandown, Shanklin and Ventnor on the Isle of
    Wight

For children

Paultons Park, Romsey
Pyramids, Southsea
Thorpe Park, Surrey
Chessington, Surrey
Marwell Zoo, Winchester
IceTrax, Poole
Splashdown, Poole
Bembom Brothers White Knuckle Theme Park,
    Margate
Robin Hill Adventure Park, Newport, Isle of
    Wight
Blackgang Chine Fantasy Theme Park,
    Ventnor, Isle of Wight

Conservation areas

AONB in Dorset, Hampshire, Sussex, Kent
    and the Isle of Wight
North and South Downs Way Long Distance
    Footpaths
Wildfowl Trust at Arundel, Hampshire
New Forest, Dorset

Theme parks and unusual attractions

Paultons Park, Romsey
Pyramids, Southsea
Thorpe Park, Surrey
Chessington, Surrey
Bembom Brothers White Knuckle Theme Park,
    Margate
Turin Shroud, Bournemouth
Terracotta Warriors, Bournemouth
Tutankhamun Exhibition, Dorchester

Historical heritage

Royal Naval Museum, Portsmouth
Mary Rose, Portsmouth
HMS *Victory*, Portsmouth
HMS *Warrior*, Portsmouth
D–Day Museum, Southsea
Royal Pavilion, Brighton
Museum of RNLI, Eastbourne
Tank Museum, Poole
Coastal Defences Museum, Eastbourne
Broadlands, Winchester, Hampshire
Day at the Wells, Tunbridge Wells
Canterbury Tales, Kent
White Cliffs Experience, Dover
Crusades Experience, Winchester, Hampshire
Osborne House, Cowes, Isle of Wight
Arreton Manor, Arreton, Isle of Wight
Haseley Manor, Arreton, Isle of Wight
Corfe Castle, Dorset

Local festivals

June	Bristol–Bournemouth Vintage Vehicle Run
August	Yachting Regatta and Cowes Week, Isle of Wight
	Southsea Show, Hampshire
	Bournemouth Regatta and Carnival
	Bournemouth Festival of Lights
	Folkestone Festival
September	Hop Picking and Beer Festival at various locations in Kent
	Hastings Day Celebrations, East Sussex
October	Canterbury Festival,
	Cider Making Festival, Shire Horse Centre, Isle of Wight

5 *South West England*

This area of England stretches from the Bristol Channel, through the Mendip Hills, Exmoor and Dartmoor to the English Channel in South Devon and Cornwall. It is covered by the West Country Tourist Board and includes the counties of:

- **Wiltshire**
- **Avon**
- **Somerset**
- **Devon**
- **Cornwall**

We shall also consider the attractions of the Isles of Scilly in this chapter since they are only 28 miles from the coast of Cornwall.

Access to South West England is by way of the M4 from London and the east, and the M5 from the north. Car ferries sail throughout the year from Plymouth to France and Spain, and there are summer services from Torquay to the Channel Islands and from Penzance to the Isles of Scilly. There are airports at Plymouth, Exeter and Newquay and a heliport for services to the Isles of Scilly at Penzance. Bristol is a major connecting point for rail services to all parts of England and Wales. The rail journey from London to Penzance takes approximately 5 hours.

The West Country receives more UK residents on holiday than any other area in Britain. In 1991, UK residents made 13.5 million trips to the West Country and spent nearly £2000 million. Overseas visitors also find the West Country attractive, with only London and the South East receiving more overseas visitors in 1991. In terms of attractions which charge admission, wildlife attractions are the most popular in the West Country, the top of the list being Bristol Zoo, Cricket St Thomas Wildlife Park in Somerset, the National Shire Horse Centre in Plymouth and Paignton Zoo in Devon.

Many of the attractions of this area, which is surrounded by water, are inevitably linked with the sea. We will consider the the following:

- natural attractions of the moors and coastlines
- seaside resorts along both coastlines
- historical heritage which spans over 5000 years from stone circles through British maritime history to Victorian times
- stately homes in an area renowned for offering relaxation in a mild climate
- industrial heritage from ancient tin mines to Clarks shoes.

Natural attractions

With the two National Parks of Exmoor and Dartmoor and extensive miles of Heritage Coastline, South West England is recognised as an area of great natural beauty. Exmoor's underlying sandstone gives it gentle contours with hidden valleys and belts of woodland. Red deer and ponies roam free and Doone Valley, the setting of

R. D. Blackmore's *Lorna Doone*, is a special attraction for tourists. Wild moorland dominates the Dartmoor National Park where most of the land is over 1000 feet above sea level, with menacing granite tors rising out of the mist. Willow and Wetlands Visitor Centre at Stoke St Gregory in Somerset gives information about one of the most important areas of wetland left in England. Designated Areas of Outstanding Natural Beauty (AONB) and Heritage Coastlines stretch right along both the north and south coasts of the peninsular.

Land's End is at the furthest point west, with its craggy cliffs falling into the sea and the famous Longship Lighthouse. The area has become commercialised in recent years but the natural spectacle of rocks and waves can still be experienced. Located 12 miles offshore and in the County of Devon, is Lundy, a tiny granite island which is 2 hours from Ilfracombe by steamer in the summer. Its rocky headlands are totally unspoilt, there are no cars on the island and the small island community of church, tavern and castle offers a refreshing change from the bustling mainland. The small hotel accommodates tourists who wish to stay longer for bird-watching and rock climbing.

Inland, caves are a feature of this part of England. The best known are the Cheddar Showcaves in Somerset with their massive limestone cliffs, deep-running caves and glittering stalactites and stalagmites. Wookey Hole Caves, 10 miles away near to Wells, are steeped in legends of witches who lived in the caves. Some of the caves are the highest-domed in the world. Lydford Gorge in Devon has dramatic potholes in the stream bed and at the end of the gorge is the 90 foot-high White Lady Waterfall.

Seaside resorts

Seaside resorts abound along both the north and south coasts of the peninsular and below we will consider some of the more popular ones.

Avon has the famous resort of Weston-super-Mare with its wide sands, piers, parks, marine parade and golf course. Two museums of note in the town are the Helicopter Museum with more than 30 machines on display and the Woodspring Museum housed in the workshops of the Edwardian Gaslight Company. The exhibits, which are arranged around a central courtyard, depict features of a typical Victorian seaside resort.

Somerset has Burnham-on-Sea and Minehead. Burnham was designed as a spa town but when that venture failed the town became a quiet seaside resort. Minehead is the brasher of the two resorts and its entertainment is supplemented by the Butlin's Holiday Camp just outside the town. On May Day each year, Minehead holds a Hobby Horse Festival. This is a smaller version of the more famous one at Padstow in Cornwall.

Devon has an abundance of resorts such as Lynmouth, Combe Martin and Ilfracombe on the north coast and Sidmouth, Dawlish, Torquay, Paignton and Brixham on the south coast. The northern resorts tend to be very picturesque with thatched cottages and old fishing ports. Clovelly, which is about 20 miles south of Ilfracombe, is the perfect example of a picturesque fishing village converted to tourism. Years ago it was a lonely, isolated one-street village. Nowadays tourists stream down the steep high street in one great mass only to be transported back up the cliff by Landrover. Torquay markets itself as the English Riviera and has a definite continental air about it. All the traditional features of a seaside resort are available as well as modern attractions such as Aqualand, the Torbay Steam Railway and Bygones, a Victorian Street complete with a forge, a pub, period rooms and authentic smells. The other southern resorts tend to be quieter, although Brixham in particular can get very congested with day-trippers.

Cornish resorts on the north coast include Bude, Newquay and St Ives, while the south coast has Penzance, Fowey and Looe. Bude is a quiet resort, popular with families and golfers. St Ives has been a haunt for artists since the days of Turner in the early nineteenth century. Newquay is the largest of the Cornish resorts, made popular by its sandy beach backed by tall cliffs and enticing caves, a very mild climate and excellent surfing facilities.

Penzance is a bustling resort with commercial as well as holiday interests while other resorts such as Looe have retained the attractiveness of small fishing villages.

The Cornish peninsula is no more than 20 miles across at some points so the attractions of the area are generally accessible from most resorts. From north to south, some of the main attractions are:

♦ Dobwells Family Adventure Park near Liskeard, which has several steam and miniature railway rides and eight themed areas with adventure play equipment
♦ Dairyland at Newquay, where visitors can watch cows being milked to music on a merry-go-round milking machine
♦ World in Miniature at Goonhavern, which is four attractions in one, with miniature famous landmarks such as the Statue of Liberty, a wild-west town, a 180-degree Cinema, and beautifully landscaped gardens
♦ St Agnes Leisure Park, which has a Super X Simulator, model dinosaurs, a circus, a haunted house and an illuminated fairyland
♦ Flambards at Helston, an all-weather attraction with a Victorian Street, a Britain in the Blitz Street, and a variety of fairground rides.

Historical heritage

Stonehenge in Wiltshire is one of the most famous prehistoric monuments in Europe. Its construction is thought to date back to 5000 years ago but it is in fact pre-dated by the site at Avebury, also in Wiltshire. The administration of both sites is shared by the National Trust and English Heritage.

Medieval times saw the building of many castles and monasteries in South West England. At Glastonbury Abbey in Somerset visitors can see extensive ruins of the first Christian Sanctuary in the British Isles, said to be the burial place of King Arthur. Buckfast Abbey in Devon has a remarkable history because, although it was founded in 1018 and the monks left during the Dissolution of the monasteries in the sixteenth

century, monks returned to the site in 1882 and the abbey is now a thriving community, selling its Buckfast tonic wine to visitors. St Michael's Mount rises like a fairytale castle out of the sea off the Cornish coast close to Penzance. It has been a priory, fortress and is now a private home. The castle is open to the public at times but tourists can always visit the village of Victorian houses which surround it.

Four cities of the South West must be singled out for their historical heritage and attraction to tourists:

♦ Salisbury in Wiltshire is clustered around its beautiful cathedral. The pattern of the old medieval streets is still visible and some of the older buildings have survived. Shopping in modern Salisbury is also a pleasure for tourists.
♦ Bath in the county of Avon is renowned for its Georgian elegance with The Circus, Queen Square and Royal Crescent being fine examples of the architecture of the period. No. 1 Royal Crescent has been restored to look as it would have done 200 years ago. It was also, incidentally, the home of the Duke of York, famed for marching his 10 000 men up the hill and down again.
♦ Bristol remembers its maritime past in the Maritime Heritage Centre where exhibits relate to 200 years of shipbuilding. The SS *Great Britain*, the first iron, screw-propelled ocean-going vessel is on display to the public. The ship was designed by Isambard Kingdom Brunel and was originally launched in 1843.
♦ Plymouth is a beautiful spacious city which was almost totally redesigned after the Blitz in World War II. The Hoe, an elevated park and walkway on the seafront gives a feeling of spaciousness, whereas the nearby Barbican has retained the old alleyways and houses of the medieval fortress town. The Plymouth Dome is a modern attraction which introduces visitors to Plymouth. Its unusual audiovisual shows are cleverly designed to interest the three main markets of UK visitors, Australians and Americans. Captain Cook sailed from Plymouth as did the Pilgrim Fathers and, as everyone knows, Drake played bowls on Plymouth Hoe while the Spanish Armada approached.

◇ **Activity:** *Responding to a letter* ◇

Research accommodation and attractions in and around Plymouth and write a suitable reply to the letter below.

24 Ash Street
Manchester

Plymouth Marketing Bureau
St Andrews Street
Plymouth

Dear Sir

I have occasion to visit Plymouth in connection with my business and I wish to take the opportunity to have a short break with my family. We hope to be in Plymouth for four days during the first week in September and would appreciate your advice with regard to accommodation and sights to see.

My wife is very keen on gardening and my son and daughter, aged 12 and 14, are quite keen on swimming but otherwise are not really sporty.

We would want two rooms in a good standard hotel, preferably with sea views.

Thank you

Yours faithfully

W. Armstrong

W Armstrong

Stately homes

Longleat in Wiltshire was the first stately home in the country to be opened to the public on a regular basis. The estate now offers a variety of attractions to rival modern-day theme parks. The Elizabethan house has fine furnishings and decorations, the Victorian kitchens include a culinary shop in the former scullery, the grounds have gardens, a maze and an adventure castle and the Longleat Safari Park with its famous elephants, tigers and lions. North of Longleat, at Calne, is Bowood House, a Georgian house with some work by Robert Adam. The gardens are beautifully laid out around the lake and children can be amused for hours in the large adventure playground.

Dyrham Park in Avon is a National Trust property which has retained many of its original seventeenth-century features. Moving south into Somerset, houses of special interest are Brympton d'Evercy, a Tudor and Stuart house near Yeovil, and nearby Montacute House, which also dates from that period and has a permanent collection of Tudor and Jacobean portraits from the National Portrait Gallery in London. Dunster Castle stands in a dramatic setting between Exmoor and the north coast of Somerset. The castle dates from the thirteenth century but the interior decoration spans several centuries. The garden is particularly interesting because of its exotic shrubs which thrive in the mild climate.

Devon has an abundance of stately homes, many of which are now in the care of the National Trust. Arlington Court near Barnstaple dates from 1822 and has a unique collection of small *objets d'art*. Buckland Abbey at Yelverton was once the home of Sir Francis Drake, and Castle Drogo, on the edge of Dartmoor, is a granite castle built by Sir Edwin Lutyens in the early part of this century. Killerton at Exeter is a plain house but has beautiful gardens with rare trees and shrubs, and Knightshayes Court at Tiverton has very ornate nineteenth-century gardens. Saltram at Plympton near Plymouth is a George II mansion which has survived with its original contents almost intact. Bickleigh Castle, former home of the captain of the ill-fated *Mary Rose*, is still in private hands and has a display on Tudor maritime history and on the *Titanic*. At Totnes in South Devon, Bowden House is the home of the British Photographic Museum, and visitors are greeted by guides in 1740 Georgian dress.

Cornwall too has several National Trust properties. Antony House at Torpoint near Plymouth is an unusual eighteenth-century house with a silvery-grey stone frontage off-set by red brick colonnaded wings. Lanhydrock near Bodmin was largely rebuilt after a fire in 1881 but still has its original gatehouse and some beautiful gardens. The mild climate of Cornwall provides ideal conditions for several gardens of note in the area. Trelissick Gardens near Truro, Trengwainton near Penzance and Trerice near Newquay are all in the care of the National Trust and are of special note for their exotic shrubs which cannot grow in other parts of England. Cotehele near Liskeard is a medieval house of interest, which also has a restored mill and cider press and buildings on the River Tamar which form an outstation of the National Maritime Museum.

Industrial heritage

The South West has a number of sites for tourists to see evidence of past and present-day industry. The earliest industry in the area was mining of tin, lead, copper and even silver. Shire horses were much in demand and they can be seen at sites in both Devon and Cornwall. Modern-day shoe and cider-making are of interest in Somerset.

Tin mining was mainly centred in Cornwall and the Cornish Engines at Redruth are an impressive reminder of the great beam engines which were used to pump water out of the mines and lift men and ore from below ground. Greevor Tin Mines at Pendeen near Penzance is probably Europe's deepest mine open to the public. Poldark Mine

and Heritage Centre near Helston has three levels open to the public, an eighteenth-century village, and films and displays in the museum. The grounds of Poldark include refreshment areas, a children's playground and a collection of working antiquities including a 40-foot beam engine.

Copper mining was centred at Tavistock in Devon, and Morwellham Quay, on the River Tamar, was the greatest copper port in Queen Victoria's Empire. The port was abandoned when the copper ran out in the 1920s but in 1970 a trust was formed to restore the buildings and open the village to tourists. Costumed guides are in attendance in the cottages where visitors can also dress up in Victorian costumes or ride into the copper mine. The visit to the mine is enhanced by a commentary from the train driver and illuminated tableaux deep in the mine.

Shire horses did much of the heavy work in past industries and there has been a revival of interest in them. The Cornish Shire Horse Centre at Tredinnick, north of Newquay, has three horse shows a day, a working blacksmith and cart rides.

Going down the mine at Morwellham Quay, Tavistock, Devon

The National Shire Horse Centre at Yealhampton near Plymouth has over 40 shire horses on a 60-acre farm.

The Shoe Museum at Street in Somerset is housed in the Clarks factory and has exhibits from Roman times to the present day. Sheppy's Cider based at Taunton welcomes visitors to their orchards, press room and museum. Ciders can be sampled and bought in the farm shop.

The Isles of Scilly

Only 28 miles from Land's End are over 150 islands, only five of which are inhabited. The largest of the Isles of Scilly is St Mary's and it covers only 4 square miles. The 2000 islanders live in a paradise of outstanding beauty and wildlife, set in a warm climate which encourages flora and fauna not seen in any other part of northern Europe. The private island of Trescoe is famous for its exotic tropical plants in the Abbey Gardens. Boat trips around the islands give visitors an opportunity to see the abundance of seals, dolphins and puffins.

The islands are linked to the mainland by ship from Penzance, with an exhibition about the islands on board during the $2\frac{1}{2}$-hour crossing. Air links are faster with a 15-minute flight from Land's End or a 20-minute helicopter flight from Penzance. Once on St Mary's the 9 miles of road can be covered by the circular bus route or bicycles and taxis are available for hire.

Activities on the Isles of Scilly include:

- golf (9 holes)
- squash
- windsurfing
- scuba diving
- fishing
- tennis
- horseriding
- dingy sailing
- water skiing
- shooting.

The peace and tranquillity of the islands are, however, their main attraction, for as Marian Bennett, the Chairman of the Isles of Scilly Tourist Board says, 'the islands' main attraction resides in what we don't have rather than what we do'.

Diagram 5.1   Summary map of South West England

◇ **Summary of attractions** ◇

Seaside resorts

Weston-super-Mare, Avon
Burnham-on-Sea, Somerset
Minehead, Somerset
Lynmouth, Devon
Combe Martin, Devon
Ilfracombe, Devon
Sidmouth, Devon
Dawlish, Devon
Torquay, Devon
Paignton, Devon
Brixham, Devon
Bude, Cornwall
Newquay, Cornwall
St Ives, Cornwall
Penzance, Cornwall
Fowey, Cornwall
Looe, Cornwall

For children

Aqualand, Torquay
Bristol Zoo, Avon
Longleat Safari Park, Wiltshire
Paignton Zoo, Devon
Dobwells Family Adventure Park, Liskeard,
    Cornwall
Dairyland, Newquay
World in Miniature, Goonhavern
St Agnes Leisure Park, Cornwall
Flambards Triple Theme Park, Helston, Cornwall

Natural attractions

Exmoor National Park
Dartmoor National Park
Heritage Coastlines
Lundy Island, Devon
AONB
Lydford Gorge, Devon
Willow and Wetlands, Somerset
Cheddar Showcaves, Somerset
Wookey Hole Caves, Somerset
Seal Sanctuary, Gweek, Cornwall
Trelissick Gardens, Truro, Cornwall
Land's End, Cornwall
Trengwainton Gardens, Penzance
Cricket St Thomas Wildlife Park, Somerset
Isles of Scilly

Theme parks and unusual attractions

Longleat Safari Park, Wiltshire
Dobwells Family Adventure Park, Liskeard,
    Cornwall
Dairyland, Newquay
World in Miniature, Goonhavern, Cornwall
St Agnes Leisure Park, Devon
Flambards Triple Theme Park, Helston,
    Cornwall
Helicopter Museum, Weston-super-Mare
Plymouth Dome

Stately homes

Longleat, Wiltshire
Bowood, Calne, Wiltshire
Dyrham Park, Avon
Montacute House, near Yeovil, Somerset
Brympton d'Evercy, near Yeovil, Somerset
Dunster Castle, Somerset
Arlington Court, Arlington, Devon
Buckland Abbey, Devon
Castle Drogo, Drewsteignton, Devon
Killerton, Exeter, Devon
Knightshayes Castle, Tiverton, Devon
Saltram, Plymouth
Bickleigh Castle, Devon
Bowden House, Totnes, Devon
Antony House, Torpoint, Cornwall
Lanhydrock, Bodmin, Cornwall
Trerice, Newquay
Cotehele, Liskeard, Cornwall

Historical heritage

Avebury, Wiltshire
Stonehenge, Wiltshire
Woodspring Museum, Weston-super-Mare,
    Somerset
Clovelly, Devon
Bygones, Torquay
Buckfast Abbey, Buckfastleigh, Devon
Glastonbury Abbey, Somerset
St Michael's Mount, Cornwall
Salisbury, Wiltshire
Bath, Avon
The Barbican, Plymouth
Maritime Heritage Centre, Bristol
SS *Great Britain*, Bristol
Mayflower Steps, Plymouth

Industrial heritage

Cornish Engines, Redruth
Greevor Tin Mines, Pendeen, Cornwall
Poldark Mine, Helston
Morwellham Quay, Tavistock, Devon
Cornish Shire Horse Centre, Tredinnick
National Shire Horse Centre, Plymouth
Shoe Museum, Clarks Factory, Street,
    Somerset
Sheppy's Cider, Taunton, Somerset

Local events and festivals

May	Badminton Horse Trials, Badminton House, Avon
	Floral Day Flurry Dance, Helston, Cornwall
	Hobby Horse Festival, Minehead, Somerset
	Hobby Horse Festival, Padstow, Cornwall
	Wesley Day Celebration, Trewint, Cornwall
	Bath Festival of Music and Drama
August	North Devon Show, Barnstaple
	Ilfracombe Carnival
September	Widecombe Fair, Devon
	British Sea Angling (Sharks) Festival, Looe
	Barnstaple Chartered Fair
	Sheep Fair, Blisland, Cornwall
November	Tar Barrel Rolling, Ottery St Mary, Devon

6 Eastern England

In this section we will consider the attractions of the two English Tourist Board Areas of East Midlands and East Anglia which include the counties of:

- **Nottinghamshire**
- **Derbyshire**
- **Lincolnshire**
- **Leicestershire**
- **Northamptonshire**
- **Cambridgeshire**
- **Essex**
- **Norfolk**
- **Suffolk.**

The area stretches from the North Sea to the Peak District National Park in Derbyshire. The River Trent winds its way through the area, and the Nene, Great Ouse, Yare and Stour make their way to the North Sea.

Access from the north and south is by means of the A1 and M1 and further access from the south is by the M11 and A12 and from the north by the A15 and A16. Access from the west is generally across country but the M6 which joins the M1 is the main route from the north west. The ferry port at Harwich has links which bring visitors from Scandinavia, the Netherlands and Germany. Fifteen minutes away by local ferry is Felixstowe with a car-ferry link to Belgium and a dozen passenger-carrying cargo links to various ports throughout the world. There are airports at Norwich, Ipswich and Southend, but the main holiday traffic uses the airports of East Midlands, Luton and Stansted. Rail links converge on Kings Cross and Liverpool Street in London, although links with the north are available through Peterborough. Ten London Transport Underground Stations are within the county of Essex, giving easy access to the capital.

Most UK visitors come to this area from Greater London and the south east. There is an even spread across the socio-economic groups among the visitors, most of whom arrive by car. East Anglia receives more than average interest amongst its visitors for activities to do with boating, swimming, rambling and bird-watching.

We shall consider the attractions of Eastern England under the headings of:

- landscape and agriculture
- coastline, wetlands and canals
- historical heritage
- famous people
- industrial heritage.

Landscape and agriculture

The Peak District National Park, the first in England, has a tremendous variety of scenery in a relatively small area. The wild moorland with rocky outcrops appeals to rock-climbers, cavers and hill-walkers, whereas the softer dales with their dry stone walls appeal to walkers, cyclists and motorists. Buxton Country Park covers over 100 acres and includes panoramic views from Solomon's Temple at 1400 feet above sea level. Shipley Country Park has nearly 600 acres of lakes, woodland, walks and bridleways.

Eastwards are the famous Sherwood Forest in Nottinghamshire and Rockingham Forest in Northamptonshire. Clumber Park, a National Trust estate in Nottinghamshire, is a good example of how the natural beauty of the landscape can be tamed giving beautiful gardens and walks. The Wolds of Lincolnshire are the last hills before reaching the flatness of East Anglia and these beautiful chalk uplands with hidden villages are designated as an Area of Outstanding Natural Beauty (AONB).

The Fens, south of the Wash, are probably the richest and flattest land in England. The rich dark fenland peat is so good that over 90 per cent of Lincolnshire is farmland. Farmers in East Anglia, however, tend to live in the towns and go out to their farms and this results in an open aspect to the landscape which is most unusual in England. East Anglia is renowned for its bulbs and flowers and the Bressingham Gardens near Thetford in Norfolk is one of the largest garden centres in the country, visited by countless tourists each year. Springfields at Spalding in Lincolnshire has over 25 acres of gardens with spring flowers. The town is the centre for the Flower Festival in May each year when a procession of flower-decorated floats parades through the streets while local houses are turned into charity stalls and tea rooms for the weekend.

The Flower Festival at Spalding, Lincolnshire

Agriculture and farming is so much part of the life of Eastern England that it has become part of the tourist scene too. Sacrewell Farm and Country Centre, 8 miles west of Peterborough, has gardens, farm trails and a large collection of domestic and agricultural bygones. At the Park Farm Tourist Centre at Snettisham in Norfolk, visitors can see farming in action and a wide selection of farm animals. Nottinghamshire too has its farm tourism at White Post Modern Farm Centre near Newark, 12 miles north of Nottingham, and the Brackenhurst College Farm Museum at Southwell. Leicestershire has Farmworld, 3 miles south east of Leicester, where displays range from rare breeds to a modern milking parlour and from vintage machinery to an audiovisual theatre. Farm holidays are offered throughout Eastern England with the Peak District winning several awards for their marketing of farm breaks.

The coastline of Lincolnshire, Norfolk and Suffolk has virtually all been designated either as an AONB or as a Heritage Coastline. This alone testifies to the beauty of the coastline and its importance to conservation and wildlife.

Coastline, wetlands and canals

It is not surprising that such an interesting coastline has given rise to numerous seaside resorts. At the mouth of the River Thames is Southend-on-Sea, further north is Clacton-on-Sea and in Norfolk there is Lowestoft and its larger northern neighbour Great Yarmouth. Many smaller resorts can be found right around the coast of East Anglia to Cromer in the north. Lincolnshire has one of the largest seaside resorts in the country at Skegness.

Southend-on-Sea has the traditional family appeal of a resort which has 7 miles of safe beach, a 100-year-old pier, excellent shopping, and entertainment for all ages, all within easy reach of London. Special children's entertainment is provided at Peter Pan's Playground on the seafront and at Never Never Land, a fantasy park where magic and illusion have been used to recreate favourite nursery rhymes and stories. Southend-on-Sea is also the venue for the Punch and Judy Festival in June each year.

Clacton-on-Sea is a very clean resort with tree-lined streets and colourful gardens. The pier is a centre for entertainment including live shows, amusement arcades, a swimming pool, shops and a pub. Special children's entertainment is provided at Magic City which has an indoor play area, children's entertainers and a licensed snooker club for parents.

Lowestoft, a modern fishing and commercial port, is also a popular seaside resort and a centre for inland boating holidays. Situated between Lowestoft and Great Yarmouth is Pleasurewood Hills American Theme Park with over 50 rides included in the admission price.

Great Yarmouth is one of Britain's most popular seaside resorts with 15 miles of golden beaches and traditional features such as the pier, Merrivale model village, the Pleasure Beach fairground and a modern swimming complex at the Marina Centre. Entertainment ranges from the circus to live variety shows and it is one of the few resorts to offer a casino. Within easy reach of the resort are facilities for golf, tenpin bowling, car-, dog- and horse-racing, and the resort itself is a centre for crown green bowls, with the climax in the Festival of Bowls in late August. There is a great variety of accommodation in the resort from the usual hotels, guesthouses and flatlets to a wide range of self-catering holiday villages on the outskirts.

Skegness in Lincolnshire has 6 miles of sandy beach, three fairgrounds, a marine zoo and farm museum as well as the usual facilities of gardens, bowling greens, theatres and ballrooms. Nearby Butlin's Funcoast World is open to day visitors and provides many extra facilities for families with children.

East Anglia lies to a large extent below sea level and the windmills and pumps which keep the sea at bay are a feature of the landscape. Several windmills are open to the public, and the wetlands, especially at Peakirk and Welney, provide opportunities to see birds such as flamingos, Andean geese and black-necked swans from South America. The canals, rivers and Norfolk Broads cater for tourists who wish to relax in the slow lane for a while. Numerous companies offer boats for short tours, day trips and boating holidays.

Inland, canals,which were crucial to the development of industrial life, are a feature of the landscape. The flight of 10 locks on the canal at Foxton in Leicestershire is a great feat of engineering. The Canal Museum at Stoke Bruerne in Northamptonshire has a colourful display which brings the 200 years of canal history to life. The Canal Museum in Nottingham offers free entrance to two floors of a former canal warehouse with displays depicting the history of water transport in the Trent Valley from the Ice Age to the present day.

Historical heritage

Eastern England is rich in heritage and stately homes open to the public. Some of the more important sites are listed below in chronological order.

Norman   Ashby-de-la-Zouch Castle in Leicestershire has impressive remains of the original Norman manor house, and its grounds were the setting for Walter Scott's *Ivanhoe.*

Rockingham Castle in Northamptonshire was built by William the Conqueror and the castle, which has been lived in continuously by the Watson family since 1530, had close associations with Charles Dickens.

Mountfichet Castle and Norman Village of 1066 is an award-winning reconstructed village on its original site at Stansted in Essex.

Fourteenth century   Haddon Hall at Bakewell in Derbyshire is possibly the most complete medieval manorial home in Britain.

Framlingham Castle in Suffolk, now in the care of English Heritage, has impressive walls and towers with later additions to the site. In 1553 it was the home of Mary Tudor.

Fifteenth century   Holme Pierrepont Hall in Nottingham is a fine Tudor manor house which has been in continuous family ownership, resulting in family furniture being retained in the house over the centuries.

Bolingbroke Castle in Lincolnshire is now in ruins, but this English Heritage site is of interest as the birthplace of Henry IV.

Sixteenth century   Hardwick Hall near Chesterfield in Derbyshire, a National Trust property, was built in the 1590s for Bess of Hardwick, the Countess of Shrewsbury. It is noted for its furniture, needlework and tapestries.

Burghley House at Stamford, on the border between Lincolnshire and Cambridgeshire has been occupied by the descendants of William Cecil since 1587. It is the venue for the Burghley Horse Trials in early September each year.

Seventeenth century   Belton House, Park and Gardens near Grantham in Lincolnshire is in the care of the National Trust. It has interesting paintings, furniture and porcelain, and a display about the abdication of the Duke of Windsor.

Audley End, an English Heritage property at Saffron Walden in Essex, is a palatial Jacobean house with a magnificent Great Hall.

Blickling Hall in Norfolk is a very orderly red brick National Trust mansion which has a notable garden and orangery.

Chatsworth at Bakewell in Derbyshire has been the home of the Dukes of Devonshire since the end of the seventeenth century. In a beautiful setting on the banks of the River Derwent, the house is filled with treasures, the garden has beautiful fountains and the farmyard and adventure playground appeal to children. In early September each year there is a two-day Chatsworth Country Fair. The number of cars parked in front of the house testify to the popularity of the Fair.

Chatsworth, Derbyshire, during the September Country Fair

Eighteenth century   Houghton Hall in Norfolk was built for Sir Robert Walpole, the first Prime Minister of England. It contains many original furnishings as well as a unique collection of 20 000 model soldiers.

Euston Hall near Thetford in Suffolk has a famous collection of Van Dyck and Stubbs paintings.

Ickworth, a Palladian house in the care of the National Trust, also in Suffolk, has an unusual 106-foot rotunda connected to flanking wings by curving corridors.

Wimpole Hall, a National Trust property in Cambridgeshire is a beautiful formal house where the servants' quarters, the stable block with heavy horses and the Home Farm all contribute to a full day out for visitors.

Kedleston Hall in Derbyshire is a superb Robert Adam house now in the care of the National Trust. The Marble Hall with 20 veined alabaster columns is particularly striking.

Nineteenth century   Belvoir Castle near Grantham in Lincolnshire, the seat of the Dukes of Rutland, was completely rebuilt in 1816. It is in a beautiful setting and its staterooms were the location for the filming of *Little Lord Fauntleroy*.

Calke Abbey in Derbyshire, an unusual National Trust property, built in the eighteenth century but full of Victorian memorabilia untouched in over 100 years, has been described as the 'house that time forgot'.

Woodhall Spa Cottage Museum is an original Victorian galvanised iron bungalow right in the centre of the inland Lincolnshire resort.

Buxton, set 100 feet above sea level in the peaks of Derbyshire, has been famous for its health-giving thermal springs since Roman times. The Old Hall Hotel dates back to 1570 and once played host to Mary, Queen of Scots who took the waters for her rheumatism. The Crescent was built as three hotels to house visitors in the late eighteenth century and the Edwardian Opera House is nowadays the home of the famous Buxton International Festival. Every July the ceremony of Wells Dressing draws tourists to the town to see the decorated wells, attend the blessing and watch a carnival procession.

Royal connections in Eastern England include Sandringham and Althorpe. Sandringham is the Queen's home in Norfolk which is open to the public, except when the Queen or any member of the royal family is in residence. Althorpe, the home of the Spencer family and where the present Princess of Wales (formerly Lady Diana Spencer) grew up, was built in 1508 and entirely redecorated in 1982. Apart from the link with the Princess of Wales, the house is also of interest for its collection of paintings by Van Dyck, Reynolds, Gainsborough and Rubens.

Links with a medieval past are strong in an area which has the university colleges of Cambridge, the ancient cathedrals of Ely and Norwich, and the Walsingham shrines to the Virgin Mary in Norfolk. Tourists can visit King's College Chapel, and try brass rubbing at Ely Cathedral.

Military associations in Eastern England date from medieval times to the Second World War. Bosworth Battlefield in Leicestershire now has a Visitors' Centre and Trail, while the site of the Civil War Battle of Naseby in Northamptonshire has relics of the battle and a miniature layout of the battlefield with a commentary. Cambridge American Military Cemetery and Memorial at Coton is a peaceful reminder of the US personnel who died during World War II. Duxford Airfield, also in Cambridgeshire, is a former Battle of Britain fighter station with hangars dating from the First World War, where the extensive collection of military aircraft includes the Concorde 01. Further north, in Lincolnshire, is the Battle of Britain Memorial Flight at Coningsby RAF Station where hangars contain the only flying Lancaster bomber in Europe as well as five Spitfires and two Hurricanes.

Famous people

Eastern England has associations with numerous famous people, just a few of whom are mentioned in alphabetical order below. Properties associated with these people are open to the public.

William Booth, who founded the Salvation Army, was born in Nottingham where the William Booth Memorial Complex is housed.

Lord Byron, the romantic poet, was born at his family home of Newstead Abbey in Mansfield, Nottinghamshire. The Abbey and grounds are open to the public during the summer.

John Constable, the famous painter, was inspired by the Essex and Suffolk landscape in the Stour Valley. Several places in this 'Constable Country' are very popular with tourists, such as Flatford Mill and, a little further upstream, Bridge Cottage which contains an information centre and exhibition about Constable.

Oliver Cromwell, the leader of the Parliamentarians during the Civil War and the Commonwealth, was born at Huntingdon, Cambridgeshire. The former schoolhouse, which was also attended by Samuel Pepys, now houses the Cromwell Museum. Another museum of Cromwell can be visited in his house in Ely.

Thomas Gainsborough, the portrait artist, was born in an elegant Georgian town house in Sudbury, Suffolk. The house is now open to the public and contains some Gainsborough paintings and contemporary furniture.

Robin Hood, the legendary outlaw, is remembered in the modern Tales of Robin Hood in the centre of Nottingham. This is a creation of special effects which takes visitors back through time in adventure cars, with commentary piped into each car.

DH Lawrence, author of *Sons and Lovers*, was born at Eastwood, Nottinghamshire. The house, appropriately furnished to the time of his birth in 1885, is open to the public.

Dick Turpin, the infamous highwayman, born at Hempstead, Essex, in 1705 and buried, with his horse, in York after his hanging in 1739, still excites interest and romance as one who robbed the rich to give to the poor. Essex County Council markets trips to 'Dick Turpin Country' taking in some of his old haunts.

Industrial heritage

East Anglia is not an industrialised area but the way of life in the fishing industry is remembered in the East Cottages of the Cromer Museum in

Norfolk and the Lowestoft Maritime Museum in Suffolk.

Essex remembers its links with the wool and silk trades in the Braintree Heritage Centre and the Working Silk Museum, England's last hand loom silk weaving mill. Modern-day Essex industry is centred on Ford's Dagenham works where visitors can have a tour of the plant.

Nottingham's links with hosiery and lace can be explored at the Nottingham Industrial Museum, the Lace Hall and the Lace Centre. The latter has an exhibition of bobbins and machinery and a selection of Nottingham lace for sale.

Lead mining in Derbyshire is described in a tour at Matlock Bath which includes a cable car ride up the Heights of Abraham and a half-mile boat trip on an underground waterway at Speedwell

Cavern. The National Tramway Museum at Crich in Derbyshire has a display of vintage trams from all over the world.

The Steel-Making Heritage Centre at Corby commemorates the importance of the industry to this area in previous times. Footwear too was important to the area as shown at the Museum of Leathercraft in Northampton. Modern day employers Carlsberg Brewery offer free tours of their lager brewing, bottling and packaging plant in Northampton.

Diagram 6.1   Summary map of Eastern England

◇ **Activity:** *Familiarisation trip* ◇

For this activity you should assume you work for either East Midlands or East Anglia Tourist Board.

Your task is to set up a Familiarisation Trip for a small group of people, all of whom may bring groups on short trips to your area in the future. The variety of interests and background of these people should be catered for in the proposed programme.

From the invitations you sent out, the following have accepted:

1   A female FE lecturer in Travel and Tourism from Southport.

2   A Cub Mistress and her husband from Doncaster.
3   Two male Scout Leaders from Oxford.
4   A woman from the Mothers' Union in a church in Telford, who will be accompanied by her mother.
5   A private coach operator and his brother from Bedfordshire who currently own five buses ranging in size from 20- to 45-seaters.

The programme should start with their arrival on the second Friday in May and finish on the following Sunday. You should include a variety of attractions within an acceptable time-scale, and accommodation each evening should be in centres in which you hope some of these people may be encouraged to make bookings in the future.

◇ **Summary of attractions** ◇

Seaside resorts

Southend-on-Sea, Essex
Clacton-on-Sea, Essex
Lowestoft, Suffolk
Great Yarmouth, Norfolk
Cromer, Norfolk
Skegness, Lincolnshire

For children

Peter Pan, Southend-on-Sea
Never Never Land, Southend
Butlins Funcoast, Skegness
Center Parcs, Elveden, near Cambridge
Center Parcs, Sherwood Forest, near Nottingham
Pleasurewood Hills American Theme Park, Great Yarmouth
The American Adventure, Ilkeston, Derbyshire
Rollerworld, Colchester, Essex
Gulliver's Kingdom, Matlock Bath, Derbyshire

Conservation areas

Peak District National Park
Peakirk and Welney Wetlands

Buxton Country Park, Derbyshire
Sherwood Forest, Nottinghamshire
Shipley Country Park, Derbyshire
Rockingham Forest, Northamptonshire
Lincolnshire Wolds
Heritage Coastline
AONB in East Anglia
Norfolk Broads

Historical heritage

Cambridge Colleges
Ely Cathedral, Cambridgeshire
Norwich Cathedral, Norfolk
Walsingham, Norfolk
Bosworth, Leicestershire
Naseby, Northamptonshire
Framlingham Castle, Suffolk

Stately homes

Sandringham, Norfolk
Althorpe, Northamptonshire
Belvoir, Lincolnshire
Calke Abbey, Derbyshire
Wimpole Hall, Cambridgeshire
Kedleston Hall, Derbyshire
Rockingham Castle, Northamptonshire
Belton House, Lincolnshire

Haddon Hall, Derbyshire
Audley End, Essex
Holme Pierrepont Hall, near Nottingham
Blickling Hall, Norfolk
Hardwick Hall, Derbyshire
Chatsworth, Derbyshire
Burghley House, Stamford, Lincolnshire
Houghton Hall, Norfolk
Euston Hall, Suffolk
Ickworth, Suffolk

Theme parks and unusual attractions

Tales of Robin Hood, Nottingham
Duxford Airfield, Cambridgeshire
Battle of Britain Memorial Flight, Coningsby, Lincolnshire
Heights of Abraham, Matlock Bath, Derbyshire
Turners Musical Merry-go-round, Wooton, Northamptonshire
Pleasurewood Hills American Theme Park, Great Yarmouth
The American Adventure, Ilkeston, Derbyshire
Gulliver's Kingdom, Matlock Bath, Derbyshire

Industrial heritage

Canal Museums in Northamptonshire and Nottinghamshire
Cromer Maritime Museum, Norfolk
Lowestoft Maritime Museum, Suffolk
Working Silk Museum, Braintree, Essex
Lace Centre and Lace Hall, Nottingham
National Tramway Museum, Crich, Derbyshire

Farm tourism

Sacrewell Farm and Country Centre, Thornhaugh, Cambridgeshire
Gressenhall Rural Life Museum and Union Farm, Gressenhall, Norfolk
White Post Modern Farm Centre, Farnsfield, Nottinghamshire
Brackenhurst College Farm Museum, Nottinghamshire
Farmworld, Oadby, Leicestershire

Speciality foods

Bakewell puddings, Derbyshire
Ashbourne gingerbread, Derbyshire
Stilton cheese, Cambridgeshire
Melton Mowbray pork pies
Buxton spring water
Turkeys, Bernard Matthews, Norfolk
English wine in Norfolk and Essex

Local events and festivals

May	Angling Fair, Chatsworth, Derbyshire
	Flower Festival, Spalding, Lincolnshire
	Boston Fair, Lincolnshire
	Oakapple Day, Castleton, Derbyshire
	The Rutland Show, Leicestershire
	Stilton Cheese Rolling, Stilton, Cambridgeshire
June	Lincolnshire Show, Grange-le-Lings, Lincoln
	Aldeburgh Music Festival, Snape Maltings, Suffolk
	Punch and Judy Festival, Southend-on-Sea
July	Buxton Wells Dressing, Derbyshire
	Cambridge Festival
August	Festival of Bowls, Great Yarmouth
	Bakewell Show, Derbyshire
	Rushbearing, Macclesfield, Derbyshire
	Carnival, Southend-on-Sea
September	Chatsworth Country Fair, Derbyshire
	Burghley Horse Trials, Lincolnshire
October	World Conker Championships, Ashton, Northamptonshire
	Goose Fair, Nottingham

7 *Central England*

Central England, from the borders of Wales and the Malvern Hills to the edge of East Anglia, and from the Midlands around Birmingham to the Downs and the River Thames, covers the tourist board areas of Heart of England, and Thames and Chilterns. The counties in this area are:

♦ **Shropshire**
♦ **Staffordshire**
♦ **West Midlands**
♦ **Hereford and Worcester**
♦ **Warwickshire**
♦ **Gloucestershire**
♦ **Oxfordshire**
♦ **Berkshire**
♦ **Buckinghamshire**
♦ **Bedfordshire**
♦ **Hertfordshire.**

Access to the area is made easy by the M6, A1 and M1 from the north, the M5 from north to south, the M4 from west to east and the M40, which runs diagonally across linking Birmingham with the M25 around London. There are international airports at Birmingham, Luton and Bristol as well as a domestic airport at Coventry. Rail links are good between London, Reading, Bristol, Oxford and Birmingham.

Tourism in this area depends very much on the natural attractions of hills, such as the Cotswolds, the Downs and the Chilterns, and rivers such as the Avon, the Wye and the Thames. Man-made attractions are also important with a good number of theme parks, many historical properties to visit, various sites connected with local industry and a great interest in gardens and garden centres. We will study the attractions of the area under the headings of:

♦ natural attractions
♦ historical heritage
♦ historic houses
♦ industrial heritage
♦ gardens and theme parks.

Compared to the rest of UK, this area tends to get an average number of British tourists, but more than the average number of overseas tourists. Only London and the south east actually receive more overseas visitors than Central England. This could be put down to the proximity of London, the good international airport links and the unique historical attraction of places like Stratford-on-Avon and Blenheim Palace. The National Exhibition Centre (NEC) in Birmingham has brought many additional tourists to the area and the list of local events at the end of the chapter shows the number of larger exhibitions and conferences which have moved their venue from London to the NEC. In general, the area tends to attract holidaymakers for short breaks rather than for main holidays.

Natural attractions

The beautiful countryside to be found throughout this area is well detailed by the tourist boards which offer walks and scenic routes to help tourists appreciate the beauty for themselves. Bedfordshire Tourist Information Centres offer Scenic Routes for motorists, and in Gloucestershire the Stroud Valley has dozens of planned walks, some with spectacular views.

The Forest of Dean, also in Gloucestershire, has facilities for walking, orienteering, and horse riding, all organised by the Forestry Commission. The nearby Wye Valley has been designated an Area of Outstanding Natural Beauty (AONB) and some spectacular views can be had from Symonds Yat, a wooded limestone outcrop some 500 feet above sea level which overlooks the River Wye twisting and turning through a deep gorge.

The gently rolling countryside of Buckinghamshire can be seen in the Aylesbury Valley, and the beechwood forests of the Chiltern Hills are easily accessible from London. The Chess Valley Walk takes visitors through the hills, and the Ridgeway Path and the North Buckinghamshire Way, both National Trails, have picnic sites and easier sections of circular routes for beginners.

The 800 acres of the Slimbridge Wildfowl and Wetlands Centre, between Gloucester and Bristol, offer bird-lovers a chance to see flamingos, geese, whistling ducks and Bewick swans. At Sandy in Bedfordshire the Royal Society for the Protection of Birds has its headquarters in over a hundred acres of open heathland, bracken and woodland where more than 140 species of birds have been recorded.

Wild-life parks are popular in this area including the world famous Windsor Safari Park in Berkshire, which markets itself as the 'African Experience'. Whipsnade Wild Animal Park in Bedfordshire has nearly 3000 animals in a 600 acre site. Woburn Abbey counts its Wild Animal Park as one of its major attractions and the Cotswold Wild Life Park at Burford in Oxfordshire has a varied collection of animals from all over the world.

Historical heritage

This area has a wealth of historical heritage from all ages in Oxford, Gloucester, Stratford-upon-Avon and Cheltenham. Roman remains are on view to visitors at the Verulamium Museum in St Albans, Hertfordshire, the site of one of the largest and most important Roman towns in Britain. At North Leigh, near Witney in Oxfordshire, the remains of a Roman Villa include a beautiful tessellated pavement.

The Oxford Story is a modern-day attraction which portrays the world of Oxford academics over 800 years. The exhibition was designed by the Heritage group which has used sights, sounds and smells in this and their other attractions at Canterbury and Tunbridge Wells. Mop Fairs in Oxfordshire and Gloucestershire, dating from medieval times, recall the days when domestic and agricultural labour was hired in September for the coming year. Nowadays the days are celebrated with fairs and local festivities, some of which are listed at the end of this chapter.

Stratford-upon-Avon is a unique historical attraction with many places associated with the life and work of Shakespeare. The Shakespeare Centre, next door to his birthplace, gives an introduction for visitors and, from outside the centre, buses run continually through the day to the homes of Shakespeare's mother, wife and daughter. The World of Shakespeare is a fascinating audiovisual presentation depicting a journey made by Elizabeth I from London to Kenilworth Castle. The performance of Shakespeare's plays are of course the main attraction in the season and the Royal Shakespeare Company's theatre is in a peaceful setting on the banks of the river.

Cheltenham Spa was an important tourist destination in Regency times and it has retained its elegance and architectural harmony to this day. Its attraction for modern day tourists is vouched for by the British and European Awards which have been given to the town.

Edwardian days are recalled in the Lost Street Museum at Ross-on-Wye where an Edwardian street of full-size shops has been constructed. The private collection in the museum contains music boxes, toys, dolls, wirelesses, gramophones, motor cycles and costumes of the period.

Victorian times are remembered in the two main open air museums at Blists Hill in Ironbridge, Shropshire and the Black Country Museum at Dudley in the West Midlands. Both of these museums use reconstructed buildings and artefacts to depict the life of ordinary working people in Victorian times. At Windsor, however, the life of royalty is depicted in the Royalty and Empire exhibition. This attraction uses waxworks in the real setting of the old Windsor and Eton Central railway station to show the arrival of Queen Victoria at the station during her Diamond Jubilee in 1897. The newsboy on the platform, the replica royal train, the very realistic Prince Albert in the waiting room and the seventy guards lined up to attention in the square all contribute to the very convincing atmosphere.

Memories of World War II are recalled in Coventry which suffered greatly from the bombing. The Blitz Experience is an animated exhibition which recalls those times with nostalgia, while Coventry Cathedral, destroyed in the blitz and rebuilt in a modern style in 1962, celebrates the new spirit of Coventry.

The antique trade flourishes in this part of England, and a particularly good place for tourists interested in antiques is Burford in Oxfordshire. This small town has an abundance of antique shops in lovely original Cotswold stone buildings. The little bridge over the Windrush in the town adds to the typical English charm which is so attractive to overseas visitors.

Historic buildings

Windsor Castle in Berkshire, the official residence of Her Majesty the Queen and the largest castle in the world, is the most prestigious historic house in the area. The public have access to the castle precincts, St George's Chapel, 16 State Rooms and an exhibition of the Queen's presents and royal carriages. Access to the entire site is, however, subject to closure at short notice as it is a royal residence.

Warwick Castle, situated just south of Birmingham, markets itself as the 'finest medieval castle in England'. The castle is part of the Pearson Group which includes Madame Tussaud's, and waxworks are used in the rooms to enhance the magnificent furnishings and decor. The dungeon and torture chamber are grisly reminders of the past and the grounds include a beautifully restored conservatory, the peacock gardens, a Victorian rose garden and an endless variety of walks.

Warwick Castle

Most of the historic houses in Central England were either constructed in the eighteenth century or largely reconstructed in the nineteenth century. Two notable exceptions are the thirteenth-century Berkeley Castle in Gloucestershire and the seventeenth-century Hatfield House in Hertfordshire. Berkeley Castle has a fine Norman keep and interesting medieval kitchens, but it is most famous as being the site where Edward II was gruesomely murdered in 1327. Hatfield House is mainly a Jacobean house but some parts date back to the fifteenth century. The present house replaced an older palace where Elizabeth I spent much of her childhood and many of the exhibits have connections with Elizabeth.

The most important eighteenth-century houses in central England are Woburn Abbey in Bedfordshire, West Wycombe Park in Buckinghamshire and Blenheim Palace in Oxfordshire. Woburn Abbey is set in 3000 acres of deer park with nine species of deer including the Pere David deer which was preserved from extinction at Woburn. The house contains the Duke of Bedford's private collection of portraits, Dutch masters, furniture, porcelain and silver. West Wycombe Park is a Palladian mansion which is richly decorated with frescoes and painted ceilings. Blenheim Palace, the country's largest private house, is the home of the Duke of Marlborough but is probably best known as the birthplace of Sir Winston Churchill. The classical mansion was designed by Sir John Vanbrugh and contains fine furniture, pictures and tapestries. The 2000-acre grounds were landscaped by Capability Brown and offer many interesting walks for the public.

Among the historic houses which were extensively reconstructed in the nineteenth century are the homes of the Rothschild family at Waddesdon Manor and Ascott House, both near Aylesbury in Buckinghamshire, the home of Disraeli at Hughenden Manor near High Wycombe and the home of the Earls of Lichfield at Shugborough Hall in Staffordshire. Sudeley Castle at Winchcombe in Gloucestershire was once the home of Catherine Parr, the last wife of Henry VIII, but the original building was largely destroyed during the Civil War. The present castle has a notable art collection and the grounds have been restored to their traditional Tudor beauty. Knebworth House in Hertfordshire has been the home of the Lytton family since 1490 but the original Tudor mansion was totally transformed in 1843. The house is particularly known for its Great Hall which contains some magnificent seventeenth-century panelling and a splendid plaster ceiling. Luton Hoo in Bedfordshire was reconstructed in 1903 by Sir Julius Wernher, a diamond magnate. The Wernher collection of Fabergé jewellery and mementoes of the Russian Imperial family make this a unique attraction.

Highclere Castle, situated just south of Newbury in Berkshire, is an excellent example of a truly Victorian stately home. It was designed by Charles Barry in the 1830s and its perpendicular architecture is very reminiscent of the Houses of Parliament, which Barry was building at the same time. Inside the house, one room is set aside for an interesting collection of Egyptian items brought back from Thebes and the Valley of Kings by the Fifth Earl of Caernarfon.

Industrial heritage

Ironbridge in Shropshire claims to be the birthplace of the Industrial Revolution and the Ironbridge Gorge Museum has seven sites connected with industry in the area. The Ironbridge itself is the centrepiece and it seems appropriate in this age of tourism that the bridge was in fact originally constructed in 1779 as a spectacular advertisement or attraction, simply to draw attention to the skills of local craftsmen with iron. At Blists Hill, the open air living museum, actors and artisans are dressed in period costume to bring to life a reconstructed village of the turn of the century. Other sites include the Tar Tunnel, the Jackfield Tile Museum, the Coalport China Museum, Rosehill House, home of a Quaker ironmaster, and the aptly named Bedlam Furnaces. The museum sites are spread over 6 square miles and visitors who purchase a passport ticket can visit each site in turn in their own time, returning to Ironbridge as often as necessary.

Open Air Museum at Blists Hill, Ironbridge

Older industries are also remembered in Central England with the unusual straw hats collection at Luton Museum and Art Gallery. Among the exhibits commemorating this local industry are hats which once belonged to Bud Flanagan and Maurice Chevalier. China and pottery-making is one of the oldest skills in the Midlands and many of the well known factories, such as Royal Doulton and Spode, have their own shops and displays. The Wedgwood Visitors' Centre at Stoke-on-Trent in Staffordshire has a video about Josiah Wedgwood, demonstrations by local craftsmen and a factory shop at the end of the tour.

Beer and cider are produced in the area and the Bass Museum at Burton-on-Trent shows the history of brewing, and various means of transporting beer, from shire horses to steam engines, and the tour ends by sampling the product in the museum's bar. Cider making is explained at the Cider Museum in Hereford where visitors can go down into the cellars to see thousands of bottles stored in racks down narrow passageways.

Cadbury World was opened in 1990, at the Bourneville Factory in Birmingham, and was an immediate success with thousands of chocaholics from all over the country. The tour starts in a simulated rain forest and includes a display showing the history of chocolate production, a packaging area where old-style machinery is used to produce and wrap chocolates, which can be sampled, and finally a chocolate shop for on-site purchases finishes the experience. On the same site is the Alternative Exhibition which displays some older machinery and various Cadbury memorabilia.

Throughout the counties of Central England there are several museums and exhibitions related to various means of transport. Shire horses can be seen at the Chalfont St Giles Shire Horse Centre in Buckinghamshire and at the Courage Shire Horse Centre in Berkshire. Rail enthusiasts can enjoy the Leighton Buzzard Narrow Gauge Railway in Bedfordshire or the Didcot Railway Centre in Oxfordshire which is the main centre for the Great Western Society. The Great Western Railway Museum is housed in an original 1883 goods station at Coleford in the Forest of Dean. Car manufacturing is one of the main industries in the area around Birmingham and the Midlands Motor Museum at Stanmore Hall in Bridgnorth in Shropshire has over a hundred cars and motor cycles including Ferrari, Porsche, Aston Martin and Jaguar. Finally, the Shuttleworth Collection of aeroplanes in Bedfordshire has some unique exhibits such as a 1909 Blériot and a 1942 Spitfire, all in perfect flying condition.

◇ **Activity:** *Slides promotion* ◇

Imagine you work for a travel promotion company called New Looks and your particular speciality is taking slides to assemble a ready-made package on a given area.

Your latest assignment is from the Tourist Boards of Heart of England and Thames and Chilterns who would like you to do a joint promotion for them aimed at the American market. You are to asked to:

* select 20 locations you would wish to photograph
* give the 20 slides appropriate titles, and
* write a brief commentary for the tape to be used with them.

Gardens and theme parks

In the year from 1988 to 1989 visits to gardens in the Heart of England increased by 22 per cent, which was the greatest increase in the whole of the UK. Since then visits to gardens have remained popular, theme parks have landscaped areas to attract more visitors and garden centres with their associated shops and entertainment have multiplied. The gardens in Central England are among the most beautiful and extensive in England and they include:

* the Swiss Garden at Old Warden in Bedfordshire where a complex landscape design incorporates some very rare and exotic trees and shrubs on a ten-acre site
* Wrest Park Gardens at Silsoe, also in Bedfordshire and in the care of English Heritage, which includes landscaping by

Capability Brown, formal gardens which were laid out in the eighteenth century, and a Chinese bridge and classical temple near the lake

- the Gardens of the Rose in St Albans in Hertfordshire are the headquarters of the Royal National Rose Society and include some colourful trial grounds which are open to the public

- also in Hertfordshire is the Capel Manor Horticultural and Environmental Centre at Waltham Cross which includes period gardens, gardens for the disabled, water features and an Italian maze

- Stowe Landscape Gardens is a National Trust property in Buckinghamshire which has six lakes and 32 follies in its 350-acre site

- the Botanic Garden in Oxford gives visitors a welcome rest from the busy city, and at nearby Wheatley are the famous Waterperry Gardens with all year round interest in its 6 acres of ornamental gardens.

Garden centres abound in the whole area but those of particular interest to visitors in Bedfordshire are the Podington Garden Centre and the Waresley Park Garden Centre where over 80 per cent of the plants are grown on site. In Hertfordshire are the Aylett Nurseries, just outside St Albans, which are famous for their dahlias, and the Van Hage's Garden Centre at Ware, which has sample display gardens and helps visitors with garden planning and design. Notcutts Garden Centre at Nuneham Courtenay in Oxfordshire is particularly popular because of its fine selection of roses. Country Gardens is a group of garden centres with outlets in Thatcham, Hungerford and Windsor in Berkshire; Aylesbury and Beaconsfield in Buckinghamshire; and Kempton in Shropshire.

With such an interest in gardening it is not surprising to find garden shows in the area. In May there is the Milton Keynes Garden Show and, at Malvern, the Spring Garden Show, while during August there is the Shrewsbury Flower Show.

The most famous theme park in the area is Alton Towers in Staffordshire which has rides and thrills for children and teenagers as well as beautifully landscaped gardens which can be viewed from above in the cable car or explored at leisure away from the excitement of the rides. In an area which is further from the sea than any other in the UK, several theme parks and water centres have been developed. These are listed in the summary on page 48.

Diagram 7.1   Summary map of Central England

◇ **Summary of attractions** ◇

For children

Alton Towers, Staffordshire
Drayton Manor Park, Tamworth, Staffordshire
John Nike Leisuresport Complex, Bracknell,
    Berkshire
Alice's Shop, Oxford
Hatfield Activity World, Hertfordshire
Coral Reef Waterworld, Bracknell, Berkshire
Windsor Safari Park, Berkshire
Whipsnade Wild Animal Park, Bedfordshire
Woburn Abbey Wild Animal Park,
    Bedfordshire
Cotswold Wild Life Park, Burford, Oxfordshire

Conservation areas

Cotswold Way, Gloucestershire
Chess Valley Walk, Buckinghamshire
Forest of Dean, Gloucestershire
North Buckinghamshire Way
Wye Valley, Hereford and Worcester and
    Gwent
Ridgeway Path, Buckinghamshire
Slimbridge Wildfowl and Wetlands,
    Gloucestershire
RSPB at Sandy, Bedfordshire

Theme parks and unusual attractions

Alton Towers, Staffordshire
Drayton Manor Park, Tamworth, Staffordshire
John Nike Leisuresport Complex, Bracknell,
    Berkshire
The Oxford Story, Oxford
Ironbridge Gorge Museum, Shropshire
The Black Country Museum, Dudley, West
    Midlands

Historical heritage

Verulamium Museum, St Albans
North Leigh Roman Villa, Oxfordshire
Stratford-upon-Avon, Warwickshire
Lost Street Museum, Ross-on-Wye, Hereford
    and Worcester
Ironbridge Gorge Museum, Shropshire
The Black Country Museum, Dudley
Royalty and Empire, Windsor
The Blitz Experience, Coventry
Windsor Castle, Berkshire

Warwick Castle, Warwickshire
Berkeley Castle, Gloucestershire
Hatfield House, Hertfordshire
Woburn Abbey, Bedfordshire
West Wycombe Park, Buckinghamshire
Blenheim Palace, Woodstock, Oxfordshire
Hughenden Manor, High Wycombe
Waddesdon Manor, Buckinghamshire
Ascott House, Aylesbury, Buckinghamshire
Shugborough, Staffordshire
Sudeley Castle, Winchcombe,
    Gloucestershire
Knebworth House, Hertfordshire
Luton Hoo, Bedfordshire
Highclere Castle, near Newbury, Berkshire

Industrial heritage

Ironbridge Gorge Museum
Luton Museum and Art Gallery
Wedgwood Visitor Centre, Stoke-on-Trent
Cadbury World, Birmingham
Midland Motor Museum, Bridgnorth,
    Shropshire
Shuttleworth Collection, Old Warden,
    Bedfordshire
Worcester Royal Porcelain, Perrins Museum,
    Worcester
Bass Museum, Burton-on-Trent
Cider Museum, Hereford
GWR Museum, Coleford, Gloucestershire
Didcot Railway Centre, Oxfordshire

Gardens

Swiss Garden, Old Warden, Bedfordshire
Wrest Park Gardens, Silsoe, Bedfordshire
Gardens of the Rose, St Albans
Capel Manor, Waltham Cross, Hertfordshire
Stowe Landscape Gardens, Buckinghamshire
Botanic Garden, Oxford
Waterperry Gardens, Oxfordshire

Local events and festivals

January	Crufts Dog Show, NEC, Birmingham
February	Boat, Caravan and Leisure Show, NEC, Birmingham
March	Shrove Tuesday Ceremony, Toddington, Bedfordshire

	Shrove Tuesday Pancake Race, Olney, Buckinghamshire
	Cheltenham National Hunt Festival, Gloucestershire
April	Shakespeare Birthday Celebration, Stratford-upon Avon
	Good Friday Cakes, Riseley, Bedfordshire
May	Beating the Bounds, Leighton Buzzard, Bedfordshire
	May Day celebration, Ickwell, Bedfordshire
	Carnival Fair, Luton, Bedfordshire
	Newbury Spring Festival, Berkshire
	Garden Show, Milton Keynes, Buckinghamshire
	Car Show, NEC, Birmingham
	Charter Fair, Stow-on-the-Wold, Gloucestershire
	Spring Garden Show, Malvern, Hereford and Worcester
	Well Blessing, Bisley, Gloucestershire
	Woolsack Races and Medieval Fayre, Tetbury, Gloucestershire
June	Rushbearing Ceremony, Pavenham, Bedfordshire
	Ludlow Festival, Shropshire
	Royal Ascot, Berkshire
	National Patchwork Champion- ships, Hatfield, Hertfordshire

	Royal International Horse Show, NEC, Birmingham
	Lichfield Folk Festival, Staffordshire
	Three Counties Show, Malvern, Hereford and Worcester
July	Regatta, Bedford
	Shaw Birthday Plays, Ayot St Lawrence, Hertfordshire
	Henley Regatta, Oxfordshire
	Henley Festival of Music and the Arts, Oxfordshire
	Art in Action Craft Fair, Waterperry Gardens, Oxfordshire
August	Football in the River Windrush, Bourton-on-the-Water, Gloucestershire
	Shrewsbury Flower Show, Shropshire
	Gatcombe Horse Trials, Gloucestershire
September	Clipping the Church, Painswick, Gloucestershire
	Statty Fair, Dunstable, Bedfordshire
	Street Fair, Charlbury, Oxfordshire
	Mop Fair, Chipping Norton, Oxfordshire
October	Ski Show, NEC, Birmingham
	Mop Fair, Tewkesbury and Cirencester, Gloucestershire

8 *North West England*

North West England is covered by the Cumbria Tourist Board and the North West Tourist Board and includes the counties of:

- ◆ **Cumbria**
- ◆ **Lancashire**
- ◆ **Merseyside**
- ◆ **Greater Manchester**
- ◆ **Cheshire.**

In this chapter we shall also consider the attractions of the Isle of Man.

The area is bounded by the Irish Sea to the west and the Pennines to the east, with the Lancashire plain, the Cumbrian mountains and lakes, and the rivers Lune, Ribble and Mersey all contributing to a great variety of scenery in this part of England.

Access to the area is by the M6 from the Midlands, the A74 and A7 from the north and the M62 from the east. Ferries operate to the Isle of Man in season from Heysham, Fleetwood and Liverpool. Manchester airport is the second largest in the country and the region also has international airports at Blackpool and Liverpool and a domestic airport at Barrow. There are InterCity rail links to Euston station in London, and frequent services to Yorkshire from Manchester.

All parts of the area receive more visitors from the UK than overseas throughout the year. Most overseas visitors come from the USA or Germany and they usually visit during July, August and September. UK visitors are mainly local to the area, with the majority of those from outside the region coming from the south east. The statistics published by the English Tourist Board lists attractions under the titles of historic, gardens, museums and galleries, wildlife, and 'other attractions'. North west England is listed as having

more of the latter category than any other area. Unusual north west attractions, which receive a large number of visitors, include the Albert Dock in Liverpool, Stapeley Water Gardens in Cheshire, and Granada Studios Tour in Manchester. Cumbria traditionally attracts visitors to its scenery and outdoor activities but in recent years it has also had the greatest increase in the UK in visits to museums. Cumbrian museums which have either recently opened or been totally renovated include the three museums in Kendal, the Cumberland Pencil Museum in Keswick, the Beatrix Potter Gallery at Hawkshead, and the Cars of the Stars Motor Museum in Keswick which has an unbelievable collection, including Trotter's van from *Only Fools and Horses*, Joey's Jag from *Bread* and the original *Chitty Chitty Bang Bang*.

We shall consider the attractions of North West England under the headings of

- ◆ natural attractions, such as the lakes and mountains of Cumbria
- ◆ historical heritage, to be found in the numerous and varied stately homes
- ◆ 'other attractions', meaning those defined by the English Tourist Board as attractions which are difficult to categorise.

Natural attractions

The Lake District National Park immediately comes to mind when we think of the natural attractions in this area. The area was very special to Beatrix Potter, one of the founding members of the National Trust, who lived in Sawrey near Windermere for many years. Within the National Park, visitors can see a great variety of scenery within a small area. Lakes, mountains, fells and footpaths are all accessible and the entire area is still very much a working environment. Some towns, such as Bowness and Ambleside, are crowded with visitors who do not venture off the beaten track with their cars, but there are still vast areas of unspoilt countryside, especially in West Cumbria. Grizedale Forest Park and Fell Foot Park at Ulverston offer the more adventurous some excellent facilities for walking, orienteering, canoeing and sailing. Throughout the entire area there are activity centres such as Hawes End on the shores of Derwentwater and the very well-equipped YMCA centre at Lakeside on Windermere.

Lake cruises are a great way to see the scenery and these can be taken on the beautifully restored steam yacht *Gondola* on Coniston Water or on the Windermere Lake Cruises, where the trip can very often be combined with a meal in a lakeside hotel. Railways too are an easy means of seeing the scenery and the Ravenglass and Eskdale miniature railway markets itself as 'the most beautiful train journey in England'. The Lakeside and Haverthwaite Railway runs steam trains from Newby Bridge during the summer season and the Settle–Carlisle Railway Line covers 70 miles of the most spectacular scenery in the north, travelling right over the Pennines.

Further south in Lancashire, the scenery changes but can be very beautiful, especially in spring and autumn. Pendle Hill for instance, whilst being famous for its association with witches, has some very pleasant views. Pennington Flash Country Park is 120 acres of lakes and wildlife just outside Wigan, and the 1300 acres of Lyme Park are within easy reach of Manchester. Delamere Forest in Cheshire has given many families a good day out and the Wirral Country Park in Merseyside includes the 12-mile Wirral Way footpath, with splendid views across the Dee Estuary. Martin

Mere Wildfowl Centre, just outside Southport, has a fine landscaped garden, a nature trail, a hide with a turfed roof and several picnic areas. Among the more unusual birds are Chilean flamingos, Falkland Islands Flightless Steamer Duck and, in winter, thousands of Pink-footed Geese.

Historical attractions

The Whitehaven district in West Cumbria claims to be the only part of England which was not ruled by the Romans but other areas of the North West have interesting relics of that era. The Senhouse Roman Museum at Maryport recreates life at the edge of the Empire on Hadrian's Wall. Most of the artefacts in the museum were unearthed by members of the Senhouse family over the past four centuries.

Cumbria has several stately homes of note which are open to the public. Holker Hall, near Cartmel, is the home of Lord Cavendish and is particularly famous for its gardens and special events, such as ballooning, which are organised throughout summer. Muncaster Castle near Ravenglass is the headquarters of the British Owl Breeding and Release Scheme and its gardens are spectacular in spring with an abundance of multi-coloured rhododendrons. The house has the outward appearance of a forbidding peel tower but the interior is filled with family treasures and heirlooms. Levens Hall, an Elizabethan mansion near Kendal, is famous for its unique topiary gardens which were originally laid out in 1692.

The Lake District was opened up to tourists with the arrival of the railway in Windermere and the towns of Windermere, Bowness, and Ambleside reflect the influence of Victorian architecture. Whitehaven on the west coast, however, remained untouched for many years, with the result that its Georgian houses and streets have been preserved to provide a pleasant change for today's visitors. Michael Moon's Bookshop and Gallery in Whitehaven, the largest bookshop in Cumbria, is an attraction in itself on a rainy day because it stocks thousands of second-hand books, from rare first editions to battered paperbacks.

The Lake District was a haven for poets and artists in Victorian times and houses associated with

View of Coniston from Brantwood, home of John Ruskin, in Cumbria

Wordsworth and John Ruskin are open to the public. Wordsworth was born in Cockermouth, went to the grammar school at Hawkshead and lived at various times in Dove Cottage in Grasmere and Rydal Mount in Ambleside. John Ruskin's home at Brantwood on Coniston Water must have the most beautiful setting of any house in the Lake District, with most rooms having superb views of the lake.

Lancashire and Merseyside have several historical properties built in the traditional black-and-white timber-framed style. Speke Hall in Liverpool, Little Moreton Hall in Cheshire and Rufford Old Hall near Southport are fine examples of this period and are all in the care of the National Trust. Croxteth Hall and Country Park, former seat of the Earls of Sefton, is in the care of Merseyside County Museums who display furniture and other items appropriate to the style of the house. The entire original contents were sold at auction in 1978, before the house passed into public ownership. Tatton Hall and Park in Cheshire is in the care of the National Trust, although the Park is maintained by Cheshire County Council. The house contains some unusual exhibits from various foreign expeditions, the grounds have

beautiful gardens and the park is the setting for several county events.

◇ **Activity:** *Themed itineraries* ◇

You have been asked by a four-star hotel in Manchester to produce themed itineraries for three two-day trips in the North West. These will be marketed by the hotel as short breaks for guests.

The suggested themes are:

* gardens
* industry at work
* stately homes.

Each themed itinerary should be designed for one side of an A4 sheet, folded in an imaginative way, and must include:

* at least three attractions
* a return to the hotel in Manchester each night
* motorists' directions from Manchester
* photographs of the attractions
* details of admission times and prices.

'Other attractions'

Many of the north west's tourist attractions come regularly at the top of the UK list of 'other attractions'. Blackpool Pleasure Beach and the Albert Dock in Liverpool have both received over 5 million visitors each year since the end of the 1980s. Entrance to both of these sites is free and, as both are situated just outside the main part of the town, parking is not a problem for visitors. Attractions in the North West which regularly receive over a million visitors include:

♦ Blackpool Tower
♦ Frontierland, Morecambe
♦ Pleasureland, Southport
♦ Stapeley Water Gardens.

Of the above list only Blackpool Tower (renamed Tower World in 1992) has an entrance charge and this is one of the oldest indoor attractions in Europe. Within the tower, apart from the thrilling ride to the top of the tower itself, there is the magnificent ballroom used for *Come Dancing*, live shows throughout the day, an underground aquarium, a children's paradise of slides and ropes in Jungle Jim's, and various arcades, shops and eating areas.

The north west's three seaside resorts of Blackpool, Morecambe and Southport are quite different in character. Blackpool is proud of its brash image of candy floss and games arcades. Morecambe is a quiet family resort with traditional small shops on the promenade which overlooks a shingle beach. Southport, in spite of having miles of golden sands, is probably better known for its splendid undercover shopping facilities in original Victorian arcades.

Stapeley Water Gardens in Cheshire has an enormous car park to cater for thousands of cars and coaches of day trippers who come to see the indoor and outdoor water gardens, receive expert advice on ponds and fountains and attend a series of talks and demonstrations organised throughout the year.

Attractions in the North West which regularly receive more than half a million visitors a year include:

♦ Liverpool Museum
♦ Granada Studios Tour, Manchester

♦ Wigan Pier
♦ Chester Zoo
♦ Knowsley Safari Park
♦ the Sandcastle, Blackpool.

The National Museums and Galleries on Merseyside are a varied group of six sites, all specialising in different aspects of history. Liverpool Museum and Planetarium has collections and exhibits ranging from the Amazonian rain forests to outer space, whereas the Maritime Museum remembers Liverpool's past glories and recreates the plight of many thousands of British and Irish citizens in the *Emigrants to a New World* exhibition. Visitors walk through dockside alleyways to enter the hold of an emigrant ship complete with bunks, tables and live actors. The hold actually sways, simulating the movement of the ship and creaking noises complete the illusion.

Granada Studios Tour is a theme park built around the original *Coronation Street* but with so many other attractions to offer that a full day is not enough to experience everything.

Coronation Street at Granada Studios Tour, Manchester

The tour includes Coronation Street, Baker Street, Downing Street and the world of the little people created for *The Return of the Antelope*. Other attractions on-site are a thrilling 3-D show, the magic of the movies experience, a real live debate in the House of Commons and the latest technology in the *Motion Master* film and ride, where the seats move, simulating the motion in the film.

Wigan in Lancashire has capitalised on an old music-hall joke and created Wigan Pier, a unique complex of restored canalside warehouses and mill buildings. Within its walls visitors can enter the living world of cloggers, tinsmiths and boltmakers; can become children again in a real live Victorian schoolroom, complete with the strictest of teachers; and can even pay their respects in a bereaved home where they are welcomed through the kitchen by the son of the house.

Several modern nuclear and space communication techniques were pioneered in north west England and some sites have been developed as attractions. Sellafield, in the Lake District, is the site of Calder Hall, the world's first industrial nuclear power station. British Nuclear Fuels Limited (BNFL) have opened a futuristic visitor centre where the work of the plant is explained in attractive surroundings reminiscent of other heritage attractions around the country. Jodrell Bank in Cheshire, home of the Lovell telescope, welcomes visitors to its planetarium, hologram exhibition, and control desk for a 7-metre model telescope.

The area also boasts two internationally famous football clubs in Liverpool and Manchester United. Both clubs have visitor centres and museums open to the public. South of the Mersey, traditional industrial heritage is remembered in several unusual museums including:

♦ the Boat Museum at Ellesmere Port
♦ the Salt Museum at Northwich
♦ Quarry Bank Mill in Styal Country Park
♦ the Catalyst Museum of the chemical industry in Widnes.

There are also several theme parks in the area including Camelot at Park Hall at Charnock Richard in Lancashire, where the theme is medieval knights but the rides are modern and thrilling. The park is owned by Granada and has close links with the American Adventure Theme Park in Derby. For one entrance price visitors can use all the rides, and attend shows as diverse as jousting and birds of prey.

Markets are a great attraction for day visitors from all over the north of England. Some of the better known weekly markets in North West England are:

♦ Ashton-under-Lyne
♦ Barrow-in-Furness
♦ Bolton
♦ Bury
♦ Chorley
♦ Fleetwood
♦ Ormskirk
♦ Stockport
♦ Tommeyfield Market, Manchester
♦ Wigan.

Isle of Man

The Isle of Man, a small island only 33 miles long and 12 miles across, is a self-governing country within the British Commonwealth with its own parliament, tax laws, currency and postage stamps. The Viking heritage of the island is remembered in the Manx Museum in Douglas as well as in the open air museum village of nineteenth-century thatched cottages at Cregneash, south of Port Erin.

The island has ferry links with Heysham, Fleetwood, Liverpool, Belfast, Dublin and Stranraer and air routes to all major mainland airports, as well as Jersey. Although the popularity of the island suffered as Mediterranean resorts developed in the 1970s and 80s, the International TT races, during the first week of June, still draw thousands of motorcycle enthusiasts each year.

The visitor's first glimpse of the island is very often the Tower of Refuge which was built in

Horse-drawn tram on Douglas Promenade, Isle of Man

Douglas Bay in 1832 to store fresh water and biscuits for shipwrecked mariners. The promenade at Douglas is lined with traditional seaside hotels and boarding houses but the horse-drawn trams on the promenade are special to the resort. About 80 horses are used during the season, with each horse averaging about four trips per day to draw the trams smoothly along on their roller bearings. The Manx Electric Railway, which runs north along the spectacular 17-mile coast from Douglas to Ramsey, is another traditional Manx means of transport. Half way along, visitors can see the 70-foot tall Laxey Wheel from where they can follow the restored pumping rod system into the upper part of the valley or take the only electrically worked mountain railway in the British Isles to the 2036 foot summit of Snaefell. Visitors who wish to travel south to Port Erin can take a steam train which covers the 15-mile journey in about an hour, with open wooden carriages giving fine cliff top views over Castletown, the ancient capital of the island.

Although the island is quite small, it can offer the visitor varied scenery, from the seventeen National Glens to recognised footpaths, including the *Raad Ny Follian* or Gull's Way, which runs right around the island with visitor centres at Ayres and Scarlett. Peel on the west coast has some fine views, as well as a medieval castle said to be haunted by the *Mauthe Dhoo* or Black Dog. Nearby Tynwald Hill is the site of the open air assembly in July which ratifies the law of the Isle of Man in a tradition which dates back to the Norsemen who conquered the island a thousand years ago. Rover tickets are available to give visitors unlimited travel on the state-owned transport on this 'island caught in time'.

Diagram 8.1   Summary map of North West England

◇ **Summary of attractions** ◇

Seaside resorts

Blackpool, Lancashire
Southport, Lancashire
Morecambe, Lancashire
Douglas, Isle of Man
Ramsey, Isle of Man

For children

Blackpool Pleasure Beach, Lancashire
Tower World, Lancashire
Sandcastle, Blackpool, Lancashire
Pleasureland, Southport, Merseyside
Frontierland, Morecambe, Lancashire
Ravenglass and Eskdale Miniature Railway,
    Cumbria
Manx Electric Railway, Isle of Man
Douglas Horse-Drawn Trams, Isle of Man
Douglas to Port Erin Steam Train, Isle of Man

Conservation areas

Lake District National Park, Cumbria
Grizedale Forest Park, Cumbria
Fell Foot Park, Ulverston, Cumbria
Pendle Hill, Lancashire
Pennington Flash Country Park, Wigan,
    Greater Manchester
Lyme Park, near Manchester
Delamere Forest, Cheshire
Wirral Country Park, Merseyside
Martin Mere Wildfowl Centre, Southport,
    Merseyside
National Glens of the Isle of Man
Gull's Way Footpath, Isle of Man

Theme parks and unusual attractions

Albert Dock, Liverpool
Stapeley Water Gardens, Nantwich, Cheshire
Camelot Theme Park, Charnock Richard,
    Lancashire
Granada Studios Tour, Manchester
Cumberland Pencil Museum, Keswick,
    Cumbria
Cars of the Stars, Keswick, Cumbria
Michael Moon's Bookshop, Whitehaven,
    Cumbria
Bridgemere Garden World, near Nantwich,
    Cheshire
Cregneash Open Air Museum, Isle of Man

Historical heritage

Senhouse Roman Museum, Maryport,
    Cumbria
Holker Hall, Cartmel, Cumbria
Muncaster Castle, Ravenglass, Cumbria
Levens Hall, Kendal, Cumbria
Beatrix Potter Gallery, Hawkshead, Cumbria
Dove Cottage, Grasmere, Cumbria
Brantwood, Coniston, Cumbria
Rydal Mount, Ambleside, Cumbria
Croxteth Hall, Liverpool
Speke Hall, Liverpool
Little Moreton Hall, Congleton, Cheshire
Rufford Old Hall, Southport, Lancashire
Tatton Hall, Knutsford, Cheshire
Abbot Hall Art Gallery, Kendal, Cumbria
Museum of Lakeland Life, Kendal, Cumbria
Kendal Museum, Cumbria
National Museums and Galleries on
    Merseyside, Liverpool
Manx Museum, Douglas, Isle of Man
Peel Castle, Isle of Man

Industrial heritage

Wigan Pier, Greater Manchester
Sellafield, Cumbria
Jodrell Bank, Cheshire
Boat Museum, Ellesmere Port, Merseyside
Salt Museum, Northwich, Cheshire
Catalyst Museum, Widnes, Merseyside
Quarry Bank Mill, Styal, Cheshire
Laxey Wheel, Isle of Man

Local events and festivals

April	Grand National, Aintree, Liverpool
May	Cartmel Races, Cumbria
	Shire Horse Parade, Liverpool
June	International TT Races, Isle of Man
	Warcop Rushbearing, Cumbria
	Appleby Horse Fair, Cumbria
	Brough Hound and Terrier Show, Cumbria
	Wirral International Lawn Tennis Tournament, Merseyside
July	Great Musgrave Rushbearing, Cumbria
	Cumberland Show, Carlisle

August	Ambleside Sports, Cumbria		Lowther Horse Driving Trials and Country Fair
	Sheep Dog National Trials, Rydal, Cumbria		Morecambe Illuminations
	Grasmere Rushbearing, Cumbria	September	Crab Fair, Egremont, Cumbria
	Woodvale Rally, Southport, Merseyside		Westmoreland County Show, Kendal
	Southport Flower Show		Blackpool Illuminations

9 Yorkshire and Humberside

The area we are considering covers the Regional Tourist Board Area of Yorkshire and Humberside and the counties of:

♦ **West Yorkshire**
♦ **North Yorkshire**
♦ **South Yorkshire**
♦ **Humberside.**

To the west the area is bounded by the Pennines and to the east by the North Sea. The Humber Bridge, the longest single span suspension bridge in the world, spans the River Humber linking Grimsby and Cleethorpes to the south with Hull and the northern parts of the county of Humberside.

The area is easily accessible from the north using the A68 and the A1, from the west using the M62 and from the south using the A1 and the M1. There are airports at Leeds/Bradford and Humberside and the port of Hull has daily sailings to Rotterdam and Zeebrugge. InterCity links give access from Edinburgh, Birmingham and London (St Pancras and Kings Cross).

According to figures published by the Yorkshire and Humberside Tourist Board, most UK and overseas visitors to the region spend their time in the North Yorkshire county, and UK visitors outnumber overseas visitors by roughly 8 to 1. Most UK visitors come from the local area, the north of England or from the south east. Most overseas visitors come from the USA and, compared with the rest of England, the region has more than the average number of visitors from Germany, Australia and Canada. Those who express a preference for any particular activity whilst on holiday put visiting friends and relatives, walking in the region and visiting heritage sites as top priorities.

Tourist attractions in this area of England may be considered under four sections:

♦ the natural beauty of the countryside, including the Pennines, the two National Parks, the Wolds and the coastline
♦ industrial heritage of cities, such as Bradford and Scunthorpe
♦ historical interest of York and the many abbeys, cathedrals and stately homes in the area
♦ traditional seaside resorts, such as Scarborough and Bridlington.

Natural attractions

There is a great variety of countryside in this area of England, as shown by the existence of two quite different National Parks. The limestone of the Yorkshire Dales has weathered over the years resulting in high fells, underground caverns and waterfalls, whereas the North Yorkshire Moors with its rocky cliffs and heather moorland can be a breathtaking sight, especially in the late summer. A network of bridleways and public footpaths gives plenty of access to the Parks. The Yorkshire

Wolds and the Vale of York have been cultivated over the centuries resulting in a truly rural atmosphere and gently rolling landscapes. The coastline gives access to marsh lands, some of which, such as the 460-acre reserve at Ousefleet in Boothsferry, are preserved by the Royal Society for the Protection of Birds. Howden Marsh offers guides for visitors to enjoy the birdlife, flora and fauna of the area. Angling is popular in Humberside and the Tourist Board has produced excellent leaflets outlining fishing areas in Goole, Hull, Scunthorpe and the West Riding of Yorkshire. The Boothsferry area also offers one of the largest networks of inland waterways in the country.

The countryside of Yorkshire is known to many people through several television series and these have been the stimulus for themed tours and short breaks. *The Railway Children* was filmed using the Keighley and Worth Valley Railway which runs into the Brontë town of Haworth. *The Last of the Summer Wine* was filmed at Holmfirth in the Dales, *All Creatures Great and Small* was filmed in Coverdale and Swaledale in the county of North Yorkshire, and *Emmerdale*, based at Esholt outside Bradford, is an on-going saga of life in the Yorkshire Dales.

Industrial heritage

Bradford claims to be the birthplace of industrial heritage tourism with their council initiative to attract visitors to the area in the 1980s. Today it is possible to shop at any of the 50 or so Woollen Mills in the area; visit Sooty and Sweep; enjoy the exhibits and IMAX circular cinema screen at the National Museum of Photography, Film and Television; and even experience an 'Asian' weekend in Bradford, sampling specialist restaurants.

Scunthorpe, a centre of steel production throughout Victorian times, now markets itself as the Industrial Garden Town. The council has financed a modern leisure centre, the town has over 1000 acres of parks and gardens and in nearby Epworth tourists can visit the Old Rectory, birthplace of John and Charles Wesley. Epworth also hosts the autumn Festival of the Plough, a

fitting venue in an area which still retains the medieval method of strip farming. Only 4 miles away at Haxey they have the summer festival of Beating the Rounds where local morris dancing troupes take part. Haxey is also the venue for a unique festival called the Haxey Hood Game on the 6th January each year. The Hood refers to one belonging to the lady of the manor of 600 years ago. Evidently she lost her hat in a gust of wind and a scuffle broke out among the locals for the honour of retrieving it. The locals now form two teams each year and battle to return the 'hood' to their local pub where it is held for the following year.

Hull emphasises its links with the rest of Europe through Rotterdam and Zeebrugge. It too has excellent leisure facilities, including an Olympic size ice rink. The Princes Quay shopping and leisure development has revitalised the dockside area, and nearby Wilberforce House, the birthplace of the slavery abolitionist, is open to the public.

Grimsby markets its smelly, fishy image positively by advertising the National Fishing Heritage Centre as the Fishing Scenter! This attraction opened in 1991 and uses special effects to recreate working conditions in a deep sea trawler, from the movement of the ship's deck to the howling wind and icy cold of the Arctic.

Heritage and history

Harrogate and York are the two main centres of heritage and history in Yorkshire. Harrogate was a spa town where people flocked even in the eighteenth century. Nowadays it is a booming conference centre with many suitable venues. For most visitors though, York is the centre of their short break or holiday. Here are historical associations from Viking and Norman times through the nineteenth century railways and up to this century's social history.

York

The Jorvik Viking Centre was built because, in the process of building a new supermarket and shopping precinct, archaeological remains of

Viking York were discovered. A Time Car now takes visitors through the underground Viking Village which has been brought to life with authentic sounds and smells. At the end of the tour some of the artefacts found during the dig have been displayed. The prize exhibit is the Coppergate Helmet, which is not in fact Viking but a superb example of an Anglo-Saxon helmet which might have been worn by a noble in Northumbria at about the time of the Viking attacks.

Clifford's Tower is the keep of the original thirteenth-century York Castle. This stone building was constructed to replace an earlier wooden tower which was burnt down in 1190 by a mob attacking besieged Jews who sought refuge in the tower. Clifford's Tower is administered through English Heritage.

York Minster is the largest medieval cathedral in Europe and it dominates the skyline in York. The Chapter House is well preserved, and is still used for church meetings, and the medieval rooms of the adjoining St William's College are open to the public. Underneath the cathedral is a display of Roman, Saxon and Norman remains and a special exhibition related to the famous painted glass of the West Window. Exhibits and specialist knowledge of the Minster are so complex that the clergy train their own cathedral guides whose skills must be updated with regular short courses.

Fairfax House, a fine eighteenth-century town house, which was once used as a cinema, is open to the public. The furniture displayed inside is, according to Christie's, one of the finest private collections of eighteenth-century furniture and clocks. The house dates from 1745 and has been restored through the sponsorship of Terry's, the York-based chocolate makers.

The National Railway Museum, a part of the Science Museum, but based in York, houses some of the earliest locomotives, Victorian royal carriages, an enormous engine weighing over 190 tons which was built in 1935 for the Chinese National Railways, and many more, including *Mallard*, which holds the world speed record for steam locomotives.

York also has the country's largest folk museum in the Castle Museum. This collection was started by a country doctor at the end of the last century as he made his round of visits and saw a traditional way of life that was still unaffected by the modern world. He began to collect items of interest, many of which other people regarded as mere rubbish. His collection extended from truncheons, bicycles and musical boxes to fireplaces, redundant farm equipment and even shop fronts. Today it is possible to walk down cobbled streets within the museum, to enter shops which have the sights and smells of Victorian days and even, bringing heritage nearer to our own day, to see a fully fitted sitting room and kitchen of the 1950s.

About 20 miles to the west of York is the cathedral town of Ripon which retains much of its olde worlde charm. In nearby North Stainley is Yorkshire's largest theme park called Lightwater Valley. For one entrance fee families can enjoy all the usual thrills and laughs of a modern-day theme park.

◇ **Activity:** *City walking tour* ◇

You have been approached by a friend who is Cub leader and in your local parish. The Cub pack will be going to York for a day trip but they are rather overwhelmed and are not sure what they should see first. Their train will arrive in York at 08.28 and they need to depart on the 21.17.

You have been asked to suggest an itinerary for the day, including meal stops, and to supply a simple map of the town which can be photocopied for each Cub.

Abbeys and cathedrals

Ripon in North Yorkshire has a cathedral which boasts the oldest complete Anglo-Saxon crypt in England. The rest of the cathedral has various styles of English architecture, and tour guides as well as Walkman tapes are available for visitors.

North Yorkshire also has more than its fair share of abbeys. The Mount Grace Priory near Northallerton is a fine example of a Carthusian monastery or Charterhouse where the monks lived in individual two-storey cells, each with its own garden and workshop.

Rievaulx Abbey, near to Helmsley, is in a beautiful setting surrounded by wooded hills. Much of the original church and buildings has been preserved and the nave is the earliest large Cistercian nave in Britain. Nearby, but unrelated, is the National Trust property of Rievaulx Terrace. This curved, half-mile grassy walk was landscaped in the eighteenth century so that the gentry could walk at their leisure contemplating the beauty of the abbey ruin beneath them, possibly one of the first examples of heritage tourism!

Fountains Abbey in Yorkshire is said to be one of the finest examples in Europe of a medieval monastery. Much of it is now in ruins but it is still possible to trace the life of the community. Fountains Abbey too became the focal point of the Studley Royal Gardens which were constructed in 1768. In summertime the National Trust presents a festival of music and light within the abbey ruins.

Stately homes

A combination of the beauty of the countryside and the profits of industry means that many stately homes have been built in this area of England.

Castle Howard, setting for the TV series *Brideshead Revisited*, was designed by Sir John Vanbrugh, architect of Blenheim Palace. The house, the largest in Yorkshire, took 30 years to complete and now contains famous collections of furniture, porcelain and paintings, including Holbein's *Henry VIII*.

Harewood House in West Yorkshire contains a rich collection of Chippendale furniture and has some of the finest Robert Adam ceilings and plasterwork in the country. The grounds were designed by Capability Brown and can be seen at their best in early summer when the rhododendrons are in bloom. The grounds also contain an adventure playground to fascinate any child and a Tropical Rain Forest Exhibition and Bird Garden.

Seaside resorts

Over 100 miles of coastline give rise to many traditional seaside resorts. The main resorts to the north are Whitby, Scarborough and Filey, and to the south of Flamborough Head are Bridlington, Hornsea and Cleethorpes.

Resorts to the north

Whitby, birthplace of Captain Cook, is a small resort dominated by the dramatic ruins of its Abbey perched on the cliff top. An unexpected attraction is the Dracula Experience wax museum on the Marine Parade. Nearby Robin Hood's Bay, a pretty village tucked into the cliff side, has a modern-day tourist attraction recalling the eerie atmosphere of smuggling days.

Scarborough first became popular as a spa town in the eighteenth century and it was one of the first seaside resorts to be developed by the Victorians. It boasts two fine promenades and beaches and the usual hotels, guests houses, a castle on the headland and miles of entertainment and fun. Of special interest to families are Kinderland adventure park for little ones, Water Splash World for all ages and, outside town on the road to Malton, the zoo and theme park at Flamingo Land. Also in the Malton area is Castle Howard, mentioned above, and Eden Camp, an unusual attraction set in an old prisoner-of-war camp which depicts civilian life during the Second World War.

Eden Camp, Malton, North Yorkshire

Filey, to the south of Scarborough, is untouched by modern bustle and prides itself on offering a traditional family resort in a beautiful setting. The surrounding cliffs, including Flamborough Head are a haven for bird-watchers, fishermen and walkers.

Resorts to the south

Bridlington is not only a bustling resort but a centre for every type of water sport. The town's Leisure World is a paradise of indoor pools, flumes and surf. Inland is the beautiful countryside of the Wolds and all along the coastline are the seabirds, flora and fauna of the Heritage Coastline. In nearby Carnaby, John Bull's World of Rock gives demonstrations of handmade rock and offers visitors the opportunity to put their own initials into a stick of rock.

Hornsea is a quiet resort with the largest natural lake in the area. Hornsea Pottery, the largest visitor attraction on Humberside, has an observation area in the factory, an adventure playground, a conservation centre, the Yorkshire Car Collection and 28 acres of landscaped gardens. Ten miles away is the colourful market town of Beverley with Georgian streets and a cobbled market. Nearby Flemingate houses the Museum of Army Transport; Hasholme is the home of the Heavy Horses, some of which were used in a television advertisement; and Walkington to the west is famous for its Victorian Hayride where heavy horses and traditional haywagons parade each summer.

Cleethorpes, south of the Humber, is a traditional resort with miles of sandy beach, an all-weather leisure centre and a full programme of entertainment throughout the summer season. On Sundays it boasts the largest undercover market in the north of England.

Diagram 9.1   Summary map of Yorkshire and Humberside

◇ **Summary of attractions** ◇

Seaside resorts

Whitby, N Yorkshire
Scarborough, N Yorkshire
Filey, N Yorkshire
Bridlington, N Yorkshire
Hornsea, Humberside
Cleethorpes, Humberside

For children

Adventure playground, Harewood,
   N Yorkshire
Kinderland, Scarborough, N Yorkshire
Water Splash, Scarborough, N Yorkshire
Keighley and Worth Valley Railway,
   W Yorkshire

Conservation areas

Yorkshire Dales, W Yorkshire
Heritage Coastline, N Yorkshire
Lyke Wake Walk, Humberside
Howden Marsh, Humberside
North Yorkshire Moors
Cleveland Way Footpath, N Yorkshire
Ousefleet RSPB Reserve, Humberside

Theme parks and unusual attractions

Lightwater Valley, Ripon, N Yorkshire
Flamingo Land, Malton, N Yorkshire
Eden Camp, Malton, N Yorkshire
World of Rock, Carnaby, N Yorkshire
Smuggling Experience, Robin Hood's Bay,
   N Yorkshire
Dracula Experience, Whitby, N Yorkshire
Museum of Army Transport, Beverley,
   Humberside

Race courses

Thirsk, N Yorkshire
Pontefract, N Yorkshire
Ripon, N Yorkshire
York, N Yorkshire
Beverley, Humberside
Pontefract, W Yorkshire
Catterick, N Yorkshire
Doncaster, N Yorkshire

Industrial heritage

Hornsea Pottery, Humberside
Bradford Woollen Mills, W Yorkshire
National Fishing Heritage Centre, Grimsby,
   Humberside
National Railway Museum, York
Hasholme Heavy Horses, Humberside

Historical heritage

Castle Museum, York
Clifford's Tower, York
Jorvik Viking Centre, York
York Minster
Fairfax House, York
Castle Howard, Malton, N Yorkshire
Harewood House, W Yorkshire
Haworth, near Bradford, W Yorkshire
Abbeys at Rievaulx, Fountains and Mount
   Grace Priory, N Yorkshire

Local events and festivals

January	Haxey Hood Game, Humberside
July	Beating the Rounds, Haxey, Humberside
August	Walkington Hayride, Humberside
September	Festival of the Plough, Epworth, Humberside

10 *North East England*

North East England forms a recognisable area with many of its own customs and dialects distinct from those of other parts of England. The Northumbria Tourist Board covers the counties of:

- **Northumberland**
- **Durham**
- **Tyne and Wear**
- **Cleveland.**

To the north is the border with Scotland through the Cheviot Hills; to the west are the Pennines; to the south the North Yorkshire Moors; and to the east the coastline with the North Sea.

Access from the north and south is by means of the A1 and the A19, and access from the west and east is by the A66 and the A69. There is an airport at Newcastle, as well as Tees-side airport at Darlington, while the ferry port at Newcastle has regular links with Scandinavia. InterCity rail services link the area to Edinburgh, Manchester, Bristol, Birmingham and London (Kings Cross).

According to figures published by the English Tourist Board, Northumbria receives the least number of visitors each year, apart from Cumbria. However, this could be misleading as the figures are based on entrances to attractions and, as we shall see below, the attraction of the north east lies in its scenery and many religious buildings which neither charge for admission nor count entrances through turnstiles. There are in fact only three attractions in the north east which regularly receive more than 400 000 visitors in a year, and these are Durham Cathedral, Beamish Open Air Museum and Preston Hall Museum at Stockton. Over the past 10 years there has been a steady, if

slow, increase in the number of recorded visits to attractions in the North East.

We shall consider the attractions of this area under the headings of:

- outdoor pursuits in the hills and coastline which surround the area
- religious heritage in an area which is regarded as the cradle of English Christianity
- historical heritage ranging from Hadrian's Wall to Victorian stately homes and living social history museums
- railway heritage in the birthplace of Robert and George Stephenson.

Outdoor pursuits

Natural beauty abounds in this part of England. The Cheviot Hills are to the north, and the Rivers Tweed, Tyne and Tees cross the area from the Pennines to the North Sea. The west of the area, from the Cheviot Hills to Hadrian's Wall has been designated as the Northumberland National Park. Stretching 40 miles from north to south and covering nearly 400 square miles, the Park gives visitors an opportunity to experience wooded valleys and fine stretches of open moorland. South of Hexham, the North Pennines is England's largest Area of Outstanding Natural Beauty (AONB). This area has been called England's Last Wilderness, with its high heather moorlands and spectacular waterfalls, the highest of which is High Force where the River Tees thunders 70 feet over massive rocks in the Durham Dales.

Kielder Water in Northumberland is Europe's largest man-made lake and facilities are available for windsurfing, water skiing, rambling and cycling. The 27 mile shoreline of the lake is set deep in the Border Forest Park and the Forestry Commission have a visitor centre at Kielder Castle from where forest walks can be organised. Throughout the National Park and the North Pennines over 300 walks are available, ranging from 1 to 6 hours duration and covering a variety of themes. Over a quarter of the Pennine Way, England's most famous long distance footpath, is within the Northumberland National Park.

Several activity centres exist in these beautiful surroundings offering instruction in a whole range of outdoor pursuits. Allenheads Lodge, south of Hexham and in the heart of the North Pennines, offers self catering or full board facilities with mountain biking, pony trekking, abseiling and rock climbing. Water-based activities are available in several centres in the Kielder Water area, and Scope Sport at Otterburn, on the edge of the National Park, offers an unusual combination of horse riding, climbing, orienteering and an assault course; all this on a farm where cheese is also made and sold in the tea room.

The long coastline with the North Sea offers numerous opportunities for bird watchers. The National Trust owns much of the coastline, including a special mile at Horden which was the 500th mile in the Enterprise Neptune appeal. Newton Pool Nature Reserve near Alnwick has over 30 species of birds, while Marsden Rock and The Leas, at South Shields, have 2.5 miles of spectacular coastline with kittiwakes and cormorants. Nearby Souter Lighthouse, a 53-room complex, built in 1871 with the first reliable electric lighthouse light, was opened to the public in 1990. Out in the North Sea, the Farne Islands have over 17 species of birds, including puffin, kittiwake and tern.

Religious Heritage

The Farne Islands are the focus for devotion to St Cuthbert, one of the founders of Christianity in Northumbria. The restored fourteenth-century chapel on the Inner Farne commemorates the death of the saint in 687 AD. Further north, Holy Island, also called Lindisfarne, which is connected to the mainland by a narrow causeway, was the base for St Aidan in the seventh century. The island is still a place of pilgrimage and the highlight of any tour is the beautiful eleventh-century ruin of Lindisfarne Priory. On the mainland further south, Jarrow was the centre for the mission of the Venerable Bede. St Paul's church and monastic site, home of the Venerable Bede, has been in continuous use for 1300 years. It has an Anglo-Saxon chancel as well as the earliest known Anglo-Saxon coloured glass window.

Hexham Abbey has a Saxon crypt, a chalice dating from the seventh century, and a Saxon bishop's stone chair. Escomb, near Bishop Auckland, has a complete Saxon church. Probably constructed about 670 AD, the church is crude and simple with irregular windows and stonework. During the construction, some stones with inscriptions were taken from the nearby Roman fort of Binchester. Upleatham church at Saltburn in Cleveland is recognised as the smallest church in England.

Gisborough Priory, at Guisborough (*sic*) also in Cleveland, was founded in 1119 by Robert de Brus and became the richest monastery of the Augustinian order in Yorkshire. Many of the buildings were destroyed in the Dissolution of the Monasteries but the Gothic beauty of the gatehouse and east end dominate the centre of the market town. Finally, Durham Cathedral is a World Heritage Site and is thought by many to have the finest example of Norman church architecture in England. It is also the site of the tombs of both St Cuthbert and the Venerable Bede. Durham Cathedral celebrates the 900th anniversary of its foundation in 1993.

Historical heritage

The North East has a second World Heritage Site in Hadrian's Wall. Built in 120 AD to mark the northern perimeter of the Roman Empire, the wall runs for 73 miles from Carlisle across the North East, to Corbridge just north of Hexham and Newcastle. Numerous forts and gatehouses have survived, one of which, Housesteads Fort and Museum, which is in the care of English Heritage, is open to the public. The site also affords impressive views of the Northumberland National Park. Parts of Hadrian's Wall still stand 20 feet high and up to 9 feet thick. Several leaflets are produced by the local councils, the National Park and the National Trust on the various sites which can be visited along the wall.

◇ **Activity:** *Interpretive skills* ◇

Your task is to produce a map of Hadrian's Wall, from Carlisle to Corbridge. The map should be large enough to display on a wall and should be illustrated with pictures of each of the points of interest.

In order to produce this map you will need to collect information and pictures from the various local councils and organisations which have an interest in the Wall. Initially you could request information from:

* English Heritage
* The National Trust
* Tynedale Council
* Northumberland National Park.

As your study expands, so should your sources of information which could include your local library and Roman History societies as well as other local councils along the length of the Wall.

You should spend about a month collecting information, two weeks collating it and a further week interpreting your information and producing the actual map.

Washington Old Hall in Tyne and Wear dates from the twelfth century but is an important part of Anglo-American heritage. It was the home of George Washington's direct ancestors and was saved from demolition in 1936 when it was restored and in 1956 given into the care of the National Trust. Apart from its American associations, it is a fine example of a small English manor house with both a Great Hall and seventeenth-century panelled rooms.

The Border History Museum is devoted to the troubled time of border warfare between the English and the Scots in the fifteenth and sixteenth centuries. The North East at that time was ruled by the Prince Bishops and was a dangerous place to live. The museum is housed in the Old Gaol at Hallgate outside Hexham and three floors of the former prison have been used to display weapons, armour, models and audiovisual presentations. The sites of two major battles at Flodden and Otterburn are within this area of the North East. Otterburn in 1388 saw a victory for the Scots and Flodden in 1513 saw the defeat of the Scots under King James IV. This was the last and most bloody battle fought in Northumberland. In those troubled times peel towers were constructed for defence on both sides. Two fine examples of peel towers can be visited at Preston Tower, north of Alnwick, with its 7-foot thick walls and tunnel vaulted rooms, and Elsdon Tower, 3 miles east of Otterburn.

As the political situation settled in 1688 Wallington House was built near Morpeth. The house was remodelled in the 1740s and is renowned for its Italian plasterwork and porcelain collection. The house is set in over 100 acres of woodlands and lakes designed by the famous Capability Brown who was in fact born in Morpeth.

In Victorian times, between 1864 and 1895, Cragside House was built near Rothbury, north west of Morpeth, for the first Lord Armstrong and it was the first house in the world to have electric lights. Lord Armstrong developed his own electricity with man-made lakes, hydraulic and hydroelectric machinery in the 900-acre park. In 1988 the Power Circuit was opened at the house to give visitors a 3-mile circular walk to see these innovative Victorian features.

The North East's Victorian past is preserved and celebrated in the Preston Park Museum, at Stockton-on-Tees, Cleveland. The park has play areas, an aviary, crazy golf and fishing. Preston Hall is a social history museum with a period street and rooms, working craftsmen, such as a farrier and blacksmith, and collections of pewter, arms, weapons, costumes, snuff boxes and children's toys.

Beamish Open Air Museum, near Chester-le-Street, south of Sunderland, has won several museum awards. In 1970 buildings were collected from all over the north east and placed in a reproduction 1900s village. Steam railway, trams and period buses provide transport around the 300-acre site where craftsmen and actors create an authentic atmosphere with the sights, sounds and smells of England at the turn of the century.

The Bowes Museum celebrated its centenary in 1992. This museum, founded by John Bowes, an ancestor of the Queen Mother, is housed in a French style chateau at Barnard Castle in Co. Durham. Not only is the architecture of the museum totally unexpected in this part of the world but the collection of paintings, ceramics and textiles displayed here are quite unique. Nearby are the notable stately homes of Raby Castle and Rokeby Park, both open to the public.

Two world famous people from the North East are Captain Cook who charted New Zealand and the east coast of Australia, and the writer Catherine Cookson. South Tyneside now markets holidays and short breaks to the Catherine Cookson Country. Places associated with her life and books can be explored around South Shields, Jarrow and Hebburn. The South Shields Museum has recreated Catherine Cookson's family kitchen and the sweet shop, described in her autobiography, which sells the toffees and peppermint humbugs depicted in her turn of the century tales.

South Tyneside is centrally situated for visits to many of the attractions already described. Ocean Beach Pleasure Park at South Shields is a traditional family amusement park with rides, video games and restaurants. Shopping is a popular tourist activity and less than 10 miles away are two of the best shopping areas in Europe at Eldon Square in Newcastle and the MetroCentre in Gateshead. The MetroCentre is open late every weekday and offers not only themed shopping malls but a 10-screen cinema, a Superbowl and the Metroland indoor theme park.

Railway heritage

The north east is the birthplace of Robert and George Stephenson and the area has preserved some unique memorabilia of the days of steam train travel. George Stephenson's birthplace at Wylam-on-Tyne in Northumberland is now a National Trust Property. The small stone tenement was built in 1760; the only room open to the public

Bowes Museum, Barnard Castle, Co. Durham

is where the inventor was born in 1781. Wylam Railway Museum details the history of railway development and the importance of Stephenson and Timothy Hackworth. The Stephenson family later moved to Wallsend in Tyne and Wear and the Dial Cottage in which they lived for 22 years, while working at the local colliery, is open to the public. The Timothy Hackworth Museum is housed in his former home at Soho Cottage in Shildon, Co. Durham. The museum has a replica of the Sans Pareil locomotive from the 1829 Rainhill Trials as well as coal drops, railway stables and a rail trial.

Railway museums abound in the North East, the most noted of which is the Darlington Railway Centre, a restored 1842 station housing a collection which includes Stephenson's Locomotion, which hauled the world's first steam passenger train on the Stockton and Darlington Railway in 1825. The John Sinclair Museum at Ford Forge near Etal in Northumberland exhibits maps, charts, diagrams and photographs and has a mock booking office.

The Stephenson Railway Museum in North Shields has the Killingworth Billy, one of George Stephenson's early locomotives, built in 1826. The Green Dragon Museum at Stockton-on-Tees in Cleveland has memorabilia associated with railways in the Stockton area plus an audiovisual show about the birth of the railways.

Throughout the area there are several sites which rank as 'firsts' in the world. The Tanfield Railway at Gateshead is the world's oldest existing railway and was originally opened in 1725. Nearby, the Bowes Railway Centre has the world's only standard gauge rope-hauled railway. Just south of Gateshead, at Stanley in Co. Durham is Causey Arch, the world's oldest surviving railway bridge built in 1725. Ten miles to the east in Sunderland is the Monkwearmouth Station Museum with a restored Edwardian booking office, platform, footbridge and siding area with a rolling stock display.

Several disused railway lines have now been turned into footpaths, bridleways and cycle tracks. Derwent Walk winds 10.5 miles south of Gateshead to Consett passing through woodlands and riverside meadows. Two visitor centres are provided along the walk at Thornley Woodlands and Swalwell. Not all lines are disused of course and the West Highlander, the luxury holiday train from London to the Western Highlands and the Isle of Mull calls at Durham each weekend in the summer to enable passengers to explore the city.

Diagram 10.1   Summary map of North East England

◇   Summary of attractions   ◇

For children

Metroland, Gateshead, Tyne and Wear
Beamish Open Air Museum, Chester-le-Street,
  Tyne and Wear
Ocean Beach Pleasure Park, South Shields
Preston Hall, Stockton-on-Tees, Cleveland

Conservation areas

Northumberland National Park
North Pennines AONB, Northumberland
Kielder Water, Northumberland
Farne Islands, Northumberland
Newton Pool Nature Reserve, Alnwick
Derwent Walk, Co. Durham
Marsden Rock, South Shields, Tyne and Wear

Theme parks and unusual attractions

Metroland at MetroCentre, Gateshead, Tyne
  and Wear
Beamish Open Air Museum, Chester-le-Street,
  Tyne and Wear
Eldon Square Shopping Complex, Newcastle,
  Tyne and Wear

Industrial and railway heritage

Wylam Railway Museum, Whitley Bay,
  Northumberland
Green Dragon Museum, Stockton-on-Tees,
  Cleveland
Timothy Hackworth Museum, Shildon,
  Co. Durham
Tanfield Railway, Gateshead, Tyne and Wear
Darlington Railway Centre, Co. Durham
Bowes Railway Centre, Gateshead, Tyne and
  Wear
John Sinclair Museum, Etal, Tyne and Wear
Causey Arch, Stanley, Co. Durham
Stephenson Railway Museum, North Shields,
  Tyne and Wear
Monkwearmouth Station Museum,
  Sunderland, Tyne and Wear

Historical and cultural interest

Hadrian's Wall, Northumberland
Bowes Museum, Barnard Castle, Co. Durham
Washington Old Hall, Tyne and Wear
Preston Hall, Cleveland
Beamish Open Air Museum, Chester-le-Street,
  Tyne and Wear
Wallington House, Morpeth, Northumberland
Cragside House, Rothbury, Northumberland
Flodden Battlefield, Northumberland
Border History Museum, Hexham,
  Northumberland
Otterburn Battlefield, Nothumberland
Warkworth Castle, Northumberland
Alnwick Castle, Northumberland

Religious heritage

Farne Islands, Northumberland
Hexham Abbey, Northumberland
Lindisfarne Priory, Holy Island, Northumberland
Durham Cathedral, Co. Durham
St Paul's Church, Jarrow, Tyne and Wear
Escomb Church, Bishop Auckland, Co.
  Durham
Upleatham Church, Saltburn, Cleveland
Gisborough Priory, Cleveland

Local events and festivals

May	Newcastle Jazz Festival
	Riding the Bounds, Berwick-upon-Tweed, Northumberland
June	Newcastle Hoppings
	Great North Fun Run
	Chevvy Chase Fell Run, Berwick-upon-Tweed
July	Alnwick Fair, Northumberland
August	Billingham International Folklore Festival, Cleveland
	Durham Beer Festival
	Cleveland International Eisteddfod (biennial)
September	Railway Carnival, Darlington, Co. Durham

11 The Lowlands of Scotland

The lowlands of Scotland stretch from the valley of Strathmore and the foothills of the Grampians, through the ancient Kingdom of Fife, to the capital, Edinburgh, and the city of Glasgow, and then south to the Southern Uplands of Dumfries and Galloway and the Borders. The counties within the area are:

- Dumfries and Galloway
- Borders
- Strathclyde
- Lothian
- Fife.

Access to the lowlands of Scotland from England is by the A74 or M74 and the A68. From the north access is by the M80 and the M90, and links between the west and east are by the M8 and the M9. There are international airports at Prestwick, Glasgow, Edinburgh and Dundee, while the ferry port at Stranraer is the link to Northern Ireland. British Rail services are available northwards to Inverness and Aberdeen, and southwards, from Glasgow via Carlisle and Crewe to London (Euston), and from Edinburgh via York to London (Kings Cross).

After London, Edinburgh with its castle, elegant shops and International Arts Festival is the most popular tourist destination in the UK. Glasgow however has increased its share of the tourist market in recent years with some very positive marketing to attract visitors to the Scottish Exhibition and Conference Centre, to the International Garden Festival during 1986 and to Glasgow as a European City of Culture in 1990. During 1989 the number of visitors to gardens and museums in Scotland was greater than to any single English Tourist Board area, apart from London. Visits to 'other attractions', which the Tourist Boards find difficult to categorise, were second only to the high number of such visits in north west England. Visits to wildlife attractions in Scotland increased by 16 per cent in 1989 but these visits are still far behind numbers to such attractions in other parts of the UK.

The Tourist Board structure in Scotland tends to be more fragmented than that in England. With 32 Tourist Boards, many of which are based on local councils, there can be a duplication of effort in some places. The county of Ayrshire amalgamated the efforts of its local district councils into one Tourist Board in 1989 in the hope of pooling resources to increase the benefits of the £200 million expected to be spent on tourism in the area in 1990. Once formed, the new Ayrshire Tourist Board became one of three pilot areas for a National Tourism Training Initiative.

We shall consider the attractions of the lowlands of Scotland under the headings of:

- the countryside, with its variety of scenery, from the valleys in mid Scotland to the long coastline of the Solway Firth and the beauty of the Southern Upland Way
- the cities of Edinburgh, Glasgow and Dundee
- historical heritage with memories of Robert Burns, several stately homes and traditional crafts such as on the Woollen Trail
- a golfer's paradise in the birthplace of the game with hundreds of courses and links from coast to coast.

The countryside

The hills, moorlands and forests of the Southern Uplands are very often bypassed as tourists make their way to the cities or highlands of Scotland. They do however offer a variety of walks, including the long distance trail of the Southern Upland Way, and the Galloway peninsular with facilities for sailing and activity holidays. The Solway Firth plays host to over 12 000 barnacle geese each winter and the Wildfowl and Wetlands Trust at Caerlaverock has outstanding hide facilities and observation towers. The Solway Coast Heritage Trail gives visitors an introduction to both the scenery and the historical heritage of this beautiful long south-facing coastline. Exotic plants thrive in the mild southwesterlies and throughout the length of the trail are castles, abbeys, little unspoilt towns and archaeological excavations of the earliest Christian times.

Within reach of Glasgow, the most industrialised city in Scotland, are some of the most visited country parks and gardens in the country.

♦ Near Motherwell, to the south of Glasgow, the Strathclyde Country Park has a wide range of water-based activities and receives over four million visitors a year.
♦ At Hamilton is the Chatelherault (pronounced *Shat-lerro*) Country Park which receives over a quarter of a million visitors a year.
♦ Further east, near the old market town of Lanark, are the Falls of Clyde and nearby is New Lanark, a World Heritage Site, where a model industrial village from the heyday of textiles has been preserved intact.
♦ Kelburn Country Park, at Fairlie in Ayrshire, is the historic estate of the Earl of Glasgow and its walks and trails lead through a collection of trees and shrubs from all over the world, with panoramic views of the islands of Cumbrae, Bute and Arran.
♦ Drumpellier Country Park at Coatbridge has over 500 acres of woodland and lowland heath. These natural features, together with the new butterfly and glasshouse complex, attracted over 360 000 visitors in 1990.
♦ The RSPB Centre at Lochwinnoch on the Largs Road has an attractive Norwegian timber observation tower with fine views of the reserve and the surrounding countryside.

The Largs Coast is less than an hour's drive from Glasgow and has some of the most spectacular scenery in western Scotland with views across to the islands of Bute and Arran. The coastline is considered one of the finest sailing waters in

Europe and Largs Yacht Haven provides modern marina and water sports facilities. The seaside town of Largs holds an exciting Viking Festival each September.

In Edinburgh, the Royal Botanic Garden offers over 70 acres of peace and greenery close to the city centre and is visited by nearly a million people each year. The garden has the largest collection of rhododendron bushes in the country, so spring is a particularly good time for a visit. However, the gardens have colour all year round, even in winter, and the exhibition hall provides excellent displays. The John Muir Country Park is about an hour's drive to the east of Edinburgh, near Dunbar. The Park, which was the first of its kind in Scotland, extends over 1700 acres which were set aside in 1976 for people to enjoy the beautiful coastline. The Park is named after John Muir, the founder of America's National Parks, who was born in Dunbar in 1838.

North of the Firth of Forth is the ancient Kingdom of Fife, an area rich in farmland, fishing and beautiful forests. The forests are managed by the Forestry Commission to provide timber for industry and recreation for the public. Graded walks are outlined, from easy ones suitable for any sensible footwear to strenuous walks, for which proper hillwalking boots are recommended. Car parks, horse trails and cycle routes are provided in all the forests.

Around Dundee, north of the Firth of Tay, the Countryside Ranger Service offers a wide selection of country walks. Within this area are several recognised country parks, including the Crombie Country Park and the Camperdown Wildlife Centre, both of which receive about 60 000 visitors a year. The Camperdown Park has a display of indigenous animals past and present, such as deer, wildcats, pine martens, brown bear, lynx, pheasants and foxes. A few miles to the north, the Monikie Country Park attracts over 150 000 visitors a year. This Park has a combination of lochs, woodland and parkland interspersed with scenic trails, picnic areas, barbecues and an adventure playground.

Cities

Edinburgh

Edinburgh Castle, with over a million visitors a year, is one of the most frequently visited attractions in the country. Within the castle, parts of which date from Norman times, it is possible to visit the apartment of Mary, Queen of Scots and the sixteenth-century Great Hall built by James IV of Scotland. The Scottish crown and other jewels are housed in the castle and annually the famous Military Tattoo is held on the Esplanade.

At the east end of Canongate is the Palace of Holyrood, the monarch's official residence in Scotland. The castle can be visited when the royal family is not in residence and the grounds are used for royal garden parties in the summer.

For the full story of Edinburgh's past, visitors should see the Camera Obscura 1850s-style show at the Visitor Centre on the Royal Mile or High Street, near to the Castle. The experience takes you through the crowded tenements of seventeenth-century Edinburgh, one of the most overcrowded places in the world at that time. Later the New Town was built north of Princes Street and its elegant squares and terraces can still be visited.

Edinburgh's past comes to life in Gladstone's Land and the Georgian House, two National Trust properties. Gladstone's Land is a six-storey house which has been furnished as a typical merchant's house of the seventeenth century, right down to the ground floor shop front with goods of the period. The Georgian House has been restored on the north side of Robert Adam's Charlotte Square. The first two floors of the house now give a very good picture of life in the grand public rooms and in the servants' quarters of a town house in the 1800s.

Princes Street is the heart of elegant Edinburgh with gardens and monuments and some of the best shopping in the country, from cashmere to kilts. The city is particularly interesting in August at the time of the International Festival and Fringe Festival and the Military Tattoo which is its final highlight.

The Royal Museum of Scotland in Chamber Street, Edinburgh, has a wide selection of exhibits and special events and received over 500 000 visitors in 1990. The National Gallery of Scotland in Edinburgh and the Scottish National Gallery of Modern Art both offer free entrance to the public and received over 100 000 visitors in 1990. The Museum of Childhood is also very popular with its collection of children's toys, books and games throughout the ages. Appealing to the whole family, the Scots Edinburgh Zoo was the fifth most popular zoo in the UK in 1990, receiving over 500 000 visitors to its 80-acre site. The zoo has been a major pioneer of serious environmentally aware zoo policies and is well regarded for its research and education programmes. Appealing to the whole family, the Whisky Heritage Centre offers a ride in barrel-shaped cars through the history of smuggling and illicit stills and the magic of Scotch whisky. Commentaries are in Dutch, French, German, Italian, Japanese and Spanish, as well as English.

Edinburgh Castle

Glasgow

Glasgow is Scotland's largest city and the third most populous city in Britain. Its cathedral was built between the twelfth and fifteenth centuries and is a fine example of pre-Reformation gothic architecture. Close by is Provand's Lordship, the city's oldest house. In the past it was host to Mary, Queen of Scots, a residence for the city hangman and later a Victorian alehouse but nowadays the carefully restored house displays furniture and pictures from various periods of the city's history. Glasgow's architectural interest in fact spans centuries because Charles Rennie Mackintosh made Glasgow a centre of Art Nouveau at the end of the Victorian era.

Glasgow's Burrell Collection of over 8000 items from the ancient world to nineteenth-century French paintings is world famous. The entire collection was a gift to the city in 1944 and it is housed in a specially designed gallery which was opened by the Queen in 1983. The McLellan Galleries were also opened by the Queen and the beautifully restored setting is host to touring and temporary art exhibitions. The People's Palace, on Glasgow Green, is dedicated to the work and leisure of the ordinary people of Glasgow. The Tenement House, a National Trust property, is a first-floor flat, built in 1892, furnished with original box-beds, kitchen range, sink and coal bunker. The flat was preserved as a 'time-capsule' by Miss Agnes Toward who lived in it from 1911 to 1965, and today it gives a vivid picture of life in Victorian times.

Dundee

Dundee, Scotland's fourth largest city, has a natural deep-water harbour on the banks of the River Tay in a lovely setting, backed by the Sidlaw Hills. The city is famous for its boat-building, especially for Antarctic expeditions. Captain Scott's ship the *Discovery* has had a chequered history but is now berthed in her home port of Dundee and can be visited by the public.

The city's maritime history is also remembered in the Albert Institute of the Central Museum and Art Gallery, in the Barrack Street Museum and in the floating museum of HMS *Unicorn*, the oldest

British built ship afloat. The changing displays on board the ship and the refurbished quarters give visitors a good idea of the hardships of sailors in the golden age of sail.

Outside the city, Camperdown House is set in nearly 400 acres of parkland with a wildlife centre, extensive woodlands and a golf course. The Dundee Flower Festival is held in these grounds each September.

◇ **Activity:** *Coach and short break destinations* ◇

Make a collection of travel agents' brochures which feature coach tours and short breaks in Scotland.

1 Using a blank map of Scotland, plot the most popular destinations.
2 Analyse the map to decide which is the most popular destination county for coach tours and short breaks in the lowlands of Scotland.
3 Read about the suggested trips and excursions in the brochures and list the most popular attractions in that county. Copy the table below and suggest a market to which each attraction would appeal.

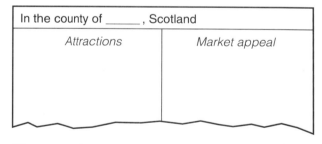

In the county of _____ , Scotland	
Attractions	*Market appeal*

Historical heritage

Scotland's maritime heritage is strong and the Scottish Maritime Museum in Irvine Harbour, once one of Glasgow's main ports, has working vessels, a unique collection of photographs, and the Tenement House which was described above. The Linthouse Engineshop recreates an authentic Victorian shipyard in a building which itself is of unique historical importance, because of the one-piece iron castings of the 40-foot high columns holding up the timber trusses.

East Neuk, in Fife, once a sea-trading centre in medieval times, has retained the maritime feel of its fishing villages. The winding streets of whitewashed cottages, tucked away in the 'neuk' or corner of Fife, are untouched by modern bustle. Apart from the very atmosphere of the villages, visitors can enjoy the Scottish Fisheries Museum and the North Carr Lightship, as well as safe, sandy beaches in the summertime. Across the Firth of Forth, in East Lothian, is the little town of Culross (pronounced *Coo-ross*). The buildings of this town have been preserved by the National Trust for Scotland and give a vivid picture of life in seventeenth-century Scotland.

Traditional Scottish industries include the woollen and the whisky trades. The Scotch Whisky Heritage Centre is in Edinburgh but there are numerous opportunities for visitors to enjoy exhibitions, bottling plant tours and tastings at plants such as the Johnnie Walker Centre in Kilmarnock. The Scottish Borders have enough woollen mills to warrant producing a Woollen Trail which includes mills, museums and woollen shops.

For many people Ayrshire is synonymous with Robert Burns. He was born in 1759 at Alloway, near Ayr, in a cottage which has been visited by many celebrities. The Land O'Burns Centre tells the story of his life and the Burns Monument is a memorial built by public subscription. There are many sites in the surrounding area which are associated with Burns' life and writings. Burns died in Dumfries where he had moved to farm at Ellisland. The farm and several other places associated with him can all be visited by the public.

Many Scottish historical properties are in the hands of either the National Trust for Scotland or the Friends of the Scottish Monuments, the Scottish version of English Heritage which promotes properties that are in the care of the Crown. Examples of such properties include:

♦ Jedburgh, Dryburgh and Melrose Abbeys, three of the four Border Abbeys, the fourth being Kelso
♦ Edinburgh Castle and Linlithgow Palace in Lothian

♦ Caerlaverock (Lark's Nest) Castle in Dumfries and Galloway, which is a real fairytale medieval castle, with a twin towered gatehouse.

Culzean (pronounced *Coo-lane*) Castle is most unusual with a strong fortress-like outward appearance, perched on the top of the Ayrshire cliffs. This imposing outward appearance contrasts sharply with the delicate interiors of Robert Adam, particularly in the circular turret rooms where the ceiling reflects the carpet and the furniture is curved to fit the walls.

Other castles and country homes abound in the lowlands of Scotland, many of them dating from the thirteenth and fourteenth centuries.

Golfer's paradise

Golf is Scotland's national game and, in Carnoustie, 12 miles from Dundee, records of the sixteenth century mention 'gowff' being played on the links. The Open was first played on the Carnoustie Championship Course in 1931.

St Andrews is probably more associated with golf than any other British city. Here in the home of golf is the British Golf Museum where famous moments can be relived through modern technology. East Lothian produces a factsheet on fourteen local courses, including Royal Musselburgh, which is reputed to be the world's oldest golf links, and the championship course at Muirfield. The Heritage of Golf Museum is in Gullane in East Lothian.

The Ayrshire coast too has its share of championship courses, including Turnberry and Royal Troon. It was at Prestwick that the first Open Championship was held in 1890. The fifteen Ayrshire courses provide not only excellent facilities but also some beautiful scenic coastal views.

North of the Firth of Forth, the district of Kirkcaldy in Fife markets itself as the 'home of golf'. Certainly the eleven courses within 12 miles of the main town witness to the popularity of the game in this area. As well as local districts promoting their golf courses, there are several tour companies in Scotland which put together either single- or multi-centred golfing holidays.

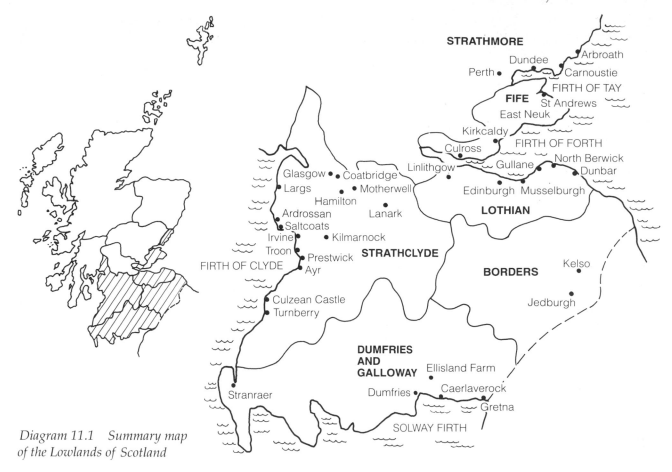

*Diagram 11.1 Summary map
of the Lowlands of Scotland*

◇ Summary of attractions ◇

Seaside resorts

Saltcoats, Ayrshire
Ardrossan, Ayrshire
Largs, Ayrshire
Gullane, East Lothian
North Berwick, Lothian
East Neuk villages, Fife

For children

Museum of Childhood, Edinburgh, Lothian
RRS *Discovery*, Dundee, Tayside
HMS *Unicorn*, Dundee, Tayside

Natural attractions

Southern Upland Way, Dumfries and Galloway
Solway Coast Heritage Trail, Dumfries and
   Galloway
Lochwinnoch RSPB Centre, Strathclyde
Caerlaverock Wetlands, Dumfries and
   Galloway
Strathclyde Country Park, Strathclyde
Chatelherault Country Park, Hamilton,
   Strathclyde
Falls of Clyde, Lanark
Kelburn Country Park, Strathclyde
Drumpellier Country Park, Coatbridge,
   Strathclyde
John Muir Country Park, Musselburgh, Lothian
Royal Botanic Garden, Edinburgh
Crombie Country Park, Dundee, Tayside
Camperdown Wildlife Centre, Dundee,
   Tayside
Monikie Country Park, Dundee, Tayside
Edinburgh Zoo

Historical heritage

Burrell Collection, Glasgow, Stathclyde
McLellan Galleries, Glasgow
Edinburgh Castle

Camera Obscura, Edinburgh, Lothian
Palace of Holyrood, Edinburgh
Georgian House, Edinburgh
Gladstone's Land, Edinburgh
People's Palace, Glasgow
Provand's Lordship, Glasgow
Border Abbeys, Borders
Royal Museum of Scotland, Edinburgh
National Gallery of Scotland, Edinburgh
Scottish National Gallery of Modern Art,
    Edinburgh
Glasgow Cathedral
Burns Heritage Trail, Ayrshire
Culzean Castle, Ayrshire
RRS *Discovery*, Dundee
HMS *Unicorn*, Dundee
Linlithgow Palace, Lothian

Industrial heritage

Tenement House, Glasgow, Strathclyde
New Lanark Model Village, Strathclyde
Scottish Maritime Museum, Irvine, Strathclyde
Borders Woollen Trail, Borders
Scotch Whisky Heritage Centre, Edinburgh
East Neuk villages, Fife
Johnnie Walker Centre, Kilmarnock,
    Strathclyde
Culross, East Lothian

Golf

St Andrews, Fife
Royal Troon, Ayrshire

British Golf Museum, St Andrews
Turnberry, Ayrshire
Heritage of Golf Museum, Gullane
Carnoustie, Dundee, Tayside
Prestwick, Ayrshire
Kirkcaldy golf courses, Fife

Local events and festivals

February	St Andrews Festival (biennial)
March	Smokies '10', Arbroath
April	Kirkcaldy Links Market
May	Highland Games, Bathgate
June	Robert Burns Festival, Alloway, Strathclyde
	Dundee Jazz Festival
	Riding of the Marches, Linlithgow
	Common Ridings, Selkirk
	International Jazz Festival, Glasgow
	'Spice of Fife' Fish Festival, East Neuk
July	Dundee Highland Games
	Dundee Children's Festival
August	Edinburgh International Festival
	Edinburgh Military Tattoo
	Marymass Festival, Irvine
September	Viking Festival, Largs
	Dundee Flower Festival
November	Scottish Motor Show, Glasgow
December	Biggar Ne'erday Bonfire

12 The Highlands and Islands of Scotland

The highlands of Scotland stretch north of a line from Perth through the shores of Loch Lomond and the Trossachs to Oban, the gateway to the Western Isles. The counties within this area are:

♦ **Tayside**
♦ **Grampian**
♦ **Highland, including the Inner Hebrides**
♦ **some districts of Central.**

We shall also consider the

♦ **Outer Hebrides**
♦ **Orkney Islands**
♦ **Shetland Islands.**

The spectacular, unspoilt scenery of this part of the UK can be appreciated on the journey following the A9 from Edinburgh to Inverness and up to John O'Groats, the most northerly point of mainland Britain. There are airports at Inverness, Wick and on many of the islands. International airports are at Aberdeen, Kirkwall in the Orkneys and Sumburgh in the Shetland Islands. The main British Rail services are through Perth to Aberdeen and Inverness. The islands are connected to the mainland with a variety of services including car ferries on the routes from:

♦ Oban to Mull
♦ Mallaig to Isle of Skye
♦ Scrabster near Thurso to Stromness, Orkney
♦ Aberdeen to Lerwick, Shetland.

Tourism in the highlands and islands is funded from a variety of sources with the Highlands and Islands Enterprise Board accounting for 20 to 25 per cent, and another 40 per cent coming from the local authorities. In 1990/91 the Scottish Tourist Board received 12.4 per cent of the grant-aid for the whole of Britain and 33.4 per cent of the grants for tourism projects, under Section 4 of the Development of Tourism Act, such grants having been withdrawn from England at the end of 1990. UK residents spent £138.50 per head on trips to Scotland in 1990/91 which was nearly 50 per cent more than the £90.62 spent per head by UK residents on trips to England. However, overseas visitors spent less in Scotland than in England, spending £428.34 for a trip per head to England but only £269.44 for a trip to Scotland.

Predictions of UK tourism indicate that inland resorts and cottages are likely to flourish in the 1990s at the expense of traditional seaside resorts. Aviemore is one area which may benefit from the new trends with its facilities integrated to rival purpose-built resorts such as Center Parcs. There has been a steady increase in the demand for cottages all year round in Scotland and owners have responded by providing accommodation with improved modern facilities.

An analysis of visits to top attractions in the highlands, from the figures published by the National Tourist Boards in May 1991, shows that none of the attractions had a million visitors, as did some in the south. However, the league table of the top 20 attractions in the highlands was as follows:

	Attraction	Number of visitors
1	Perth Leisure Pool	662 263
2	Loch Ness Monster Exhibition	350 000
3	Aberdeen Art Gallery	346 757
4	Storybook Glen, Maryculter	250 000
5	Regimental Museum, Stirling	200 000
6	Aden Country Park, Mintlaw	189 907
7	Inverness Museum and Art Gallery	189 722
8	Haddo Country Park, Ellon	180 000
9	Urquhart Castle, Loch Ness	178 415
10	Blair Castle, Pitlochry	170 554
11	Blairdrummond Safari Park	166 636
12	Glencoe Visitor Centre	166 064
13	Stirling Castle	164 734
14	Glenturret Distillery	152 518
15	Baxter's, Fochabers	150 400
16	Glenmore Forest Park, Aviemore	150 000
17	Glenfiddich Distillery	135 131
18	Stuart Strathearn Crystal, Crieff	130 000
19	Inverewe Gardens, Gairloch	129 486
20	Clan Donald Centre, Skye	120 000

We shall consider the attractions of the highlands under the headings of:

♦ natural attractions, with Areas of Outstanding Natural Beauty (AONB), forests and country parks
♦ historical attractions, such as ancient castles, city museums and centres commemorating historic battles
♦ traditional attractions, in which we will include topics as diverse as whisky, crystal and the Loch Ness monster.

We shall consider the attractions of the islands at the end of the chapter.

Natural attractions

The road traffic nightmares and motorway tailback stories of England are another world from the highlands of Scotland. The genuine green tourism of the highlands is now recognised as a marketing strength, as more people are drawn to the beauty and simplicity of a way of life totally different from the pressures of city life. Pony trekking, hill walking and angling are widely available. Diagram 2.3 on page 9 shows the extent of land set aside as AONB and Forest Parks.

Caithness and Sutherland in Highland is the most northerly part of mainland Britain and is regarded by many as the last great wilderness in Europe. Several companies arrange personalised tours and weekends at estates where visitors are entertained as house guests with stalking, fishing and clay pigeon shooting included in the package. Inverewe Garden at Poolewe, 6 miles north east of Gairloch is a remarkable garden of rare and subtropical plants on the northern shore of Loch Maree.

The Great Glen, a fault line from Inverness to Fort William, forms a coast-to-coast valley whose lochs are connected by the Caledonian Canal, and which provides a centre for watersports and cruising. Inverness has long been regarded as the 'capital of the highlands' and is the gateway to the Cairngorms, the tragic battlefield of Culloden and Loch Ness with its stories of monsters dating back to the seventh century. Loch Ness has in fact twice the average depth of the North Sea. Fort William is the gateway for climbers to Ben Nevis, Britain's highest mountain at 4406 feet (1344 m). The West Highland steam train which runs from Fort William to Mallaig has beautiful views along the shores of Loch Linnhe.

The North East Coastal Trail guides visitors through picturesque harbours and fishing ports with a backdrop of rugged cliffs from Inverness, through Aberdeen to Dundee. On the northern strip of the trail, Nairn is a golfer's centre and Pennan, the location for the film *Local Hero*, is probably unique in the whole country in having a telephone box as a listed building. Aden Country Park near Mintlaw in Grampian has 200 acres of woodland and open country with footpaths, nature trails and a countryside ranger service. Fifteen miles to the south is Haddo Country Park run by Grampian Regional Council in the former grounds of Haddo House. Storybook Glen at Maryculter, just south of Aberdeen, is a children's fantasy land set in 20 acres of flowers, plants, trees and waterfalls.

The Glenmore Forest Park in Aviemore increased its visitors in the year 1990/91 by 87 per cent to

150 000 and this reflects the growing importance of tourism in this part of the highlands. The centre at Aviemore is well established as a ski resort and offers a variety of additional facilities including:

- cinema
- swimming pool
- saunas
- artificial ski slope
- discos
- theatre
- ice rink
- solarium
- go-karts
- restaurants.

The Strathspey steam railway covers the 5 miles from Boat of Garten to Aviemore overlooked by the majesty of the Cairngorms. Ski centres are also developing at Glencoe, the Nevis range, Glenshee, Cairngorms and the Lecht.

To the south, Blairdrummond Safari Park in Central attracts visitors from both the highlands and lowlands to see wild animals in natural surroundings. The lion and tiger reserve with its aerial walkway is particularly popular.

Historical attractions

The museums and art galleries of Inverness and Aberdeen draw large numbers of visitors. Aberdeen Art Gallery has an outstanding collection of modern paintings and hosts special events and exhibitions throughout the year. Aberdeen, known as 'the granite city' because of the colour of its buildings, has enjoyed prosperity from North Sea oil and also offers a selection of seaside attractions along its 2 miles of sandy beach.

The Highland Folk Museum at Kingussie, about 30 miles south of Inverness, has a reconstructed Hebridean mill and a primitive black house as part of its open air exhibits. Further north the Tain and District Museum and Clan Ross Centre attracts over 100 000 visitors a year to see its unique collection of ancient silver, early charters and historic photographs.

Glencoe, south of Fort William, is best known as the scene of the massacre of February 1692 but is also a centre for climbing, walking and wildlife, including red deer and golden eagles. The Glencoe Visitor Centre at the north end of the glen provides information on walks and a ranger service. Culloden Moor, east of Inverness, is the site of the

last battle on the British mainland in April 1746 and the Visitor Centre has an audiovisual display in six languages about the rout of Bonnie Prince Charlie by the forces of the Duke of Cumberland. The Clan Donald Centre on the Isle of Skye houses the Museum of the Isles and, from there, a countryside ranger service offers a summer programme of walks, talks and children's afternoons.

Castles abound in the highlands with the most popular being the remains of Urquhart Castle overlooking Loch Ness, Blair Castle at Pitlochry in Perthshire, Tayside and Stirling Castle, in Central, the scene of many events in Scotland's history. The Regimental Museum of the Argyll and Sutherland Highlanders is housed in King James V's Palace in Stirling Castle and it has a fine collection of regimental silver and plate, colours, banners, paintings and uniforms. To the west of Aberdeen several castles are marketed together as the Castle Trail. The nine castles vary from the medieval ruin of Kildrummy Castle to the refurbished splendour of Fyvie Castle.

The Queen spends each August in the highlands at Queen Victoria's retreat in Balmoral Castle in Grampian. Parts of the castle are open to the public from May to July and the surrounding area is now marketed as the Victorian Heritage by Kincardine and Deeside Tourist Board. Glamis Castle in Tayside, the splendid turreted childhood home of the Queen Mother, has also gained in popularity over the years.

Traditional attractions

The official Loch Ness Monster Exhibition at Drumnadrochit draws crowds to wonder at the traditions and stories to do with the subject over the centuries. The multi-media modern presentation lasts 40 minutes and tells the story from prehistoric times.

Whisky is associated with Scotland throughout the world and there are numerous distilleries where the public can watch the process and taste the results. Some of the best known distilleries are included in the 70-mile Whisky Trail in Speyside, 50 miles south of Inverness. It is marketed in six languages and the distilleries include the

Glenfiddich, the Glen Grant and the Cardhu. The Glenturret distillery at Crieff in Tayside is the oldest in Scotland and still uses the pure water of the Turret Burn to make its world famous whiskies.

The Scottish Quality Trail also includes the Glenfiddich distillery as well as a visit to Baxter's of Speyside Visitor Centre at Fochabers. Visitors can see the Victorian kitchen where the famous soups were first made, the Old Shop Museum and take a guided tour through the modern factory. Tourists can make another factory visit in Tayside to see glassmaking and engraving at Stuart Strathearn in Crieff, Perthshire.

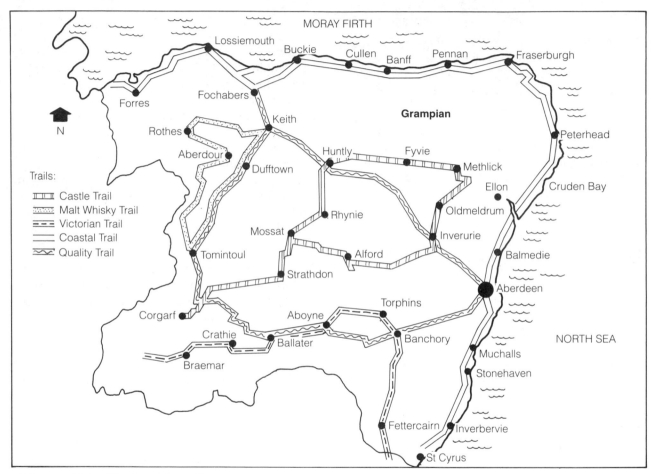

Diagram 12.1   The Scottish Trails

◊ **Activity:** *Route planning* ◊

Construct an itinerary for a Scottish touring holiday for a family of four (two adults and two children, aged 11 and 13).

The tour should start and finish in Edinburgh where they have arrived by motorail, and should last no longer than three weeks. You may choose the time of year in which they are travelling.

Your itinerary should include a map, the route, a description of places of interest and suggested overnight stops. Your clients should be able to see a variety of scenery and places, without having to spend each night in a different hotel or guesthouse.

Useful source materials for this activity are:

*   brochures on skiing in Scotland
*   publicity material from the Scottish Regional Tourist Boards
*   AA books and atlases.

81

Scottish Islands

Outer Hebrides

The Outer Hebrides or Western Isles take their name from the old Norse word *Havbredey* meaning the isle on the edge of the sea. This group of islands, 130 miles long, lies off the west coast of Scotland and is a paradise for ornithologists, artists, photographers and anglers. The landscape is barren and rugged but the Gaelic speaking people, with their strong religious beliefs, make visitors very welcome.

Lewis, the most northerly and largest of the islands, has rolling moorland and low lying hills. Historical interest on the island ranges from the standing stones at Callanish and the 30-foot high broch or tower at Dun Carloway to the Black House Museum at Arrol which depicts a traditional Hebridean dwelling built without mortar and roofed with thatch. This house retains many of its original furnishings which add to the authenticity of the experience. Nearby Harris island, as well as being famous for its tweed, is the most mountainous of the group and is ideal for climbers, hill walkers and for those wishing to see a golden eagle.

The islands of North Uist, Benbecula and South Uist are connected by bridges and causeways. North Uist is a maze of trout-filled lochs and inlets; Benbecula is also an angler's paradise, and South Uist has a bird sanctuary at Loch Druidibeg and a Black House, similar to the one on Lewis, at Eochar.

Further south, the island of Barra has over a thousand identified wild flowers and nearby Eriskay was the setting for Sir Compton Mackenzie's novel *Whisky Galore*.

Orkney Islands

The 67 islands in this group are only 6 miles north of the top of mainland Scotland, but they are on the same latitude as St Petersburg and southern Greenland. The mild climate comes as a surprise to some tourists and so do the spectacular sunsets during the longest evenings in May and June. Only eighteen of the islands are inhabited, with the largest being called Mainland, although its Viking name was *Hrossey* or Horse Island. Most of the islands are fertile with low rounded hills and a prosperous community, with the exception of Hoy which has 1000-foot high cliffs and the isolated stack known as the Old Man of Hoy.

In 1989 the Orkney Islands first passed their target of 100 000 visitors in a year. The islands are so popular with anglers and ornithologists that there are published guides to the islands for both. The Viking interest of the islands is predated by the Picts and Celts, making them of great interest to archaeologists. Skara Brae on Mainland has well preserved Stone Age houses with stone beds, cupboards and fireplaces. More recent history is remembered in Kirkwall, the capital, in Tankerness House, a museum of Orkney life, and also in Carrigall Farm Museum which is a preserved farmstead.

To the south of Mainland, Scapa Flow is the site of a North Sea oil terminal and its deep harbour saw much activity during the Second World War. Italian prisoners of war built the Churchill anti-submarine barriers in 1943 and in their spare time they converted two Nissen huts into a Catholic church. The light fittings of the church were made from corned beef tins, the altar was moulded in concrete and the rood screen was fashioned from oil drums and the combined effect is still of interest to visitors.

Shetland Islands

The entire archipelago of the Shetlands is roughly 100 miles by 50 miles. Very often they are shown in a little box on a map which hides the fact that Lerwick, the capital, is about 200 miles north of Aberdeen and the same distance west of Bergen in Norway. There are about 100 islands in the group, only 15 of which are inhabited. On these islands you are never more than 3 miles from the sea and fine white sandy beaches. The 24 000 inhabitants and their visitors enjoy a temperate climate, warmed by the Gulf Stream, but they also have to endure dramatic changes in the weather, sometimes within the same 24-hour period. At the end of June the sun shines for almost 19 hours in a day and in autumn there are dramatic sunsets with the *Aurora Borealis*, or northern lights, dancing in the sky. In both seasons visitors can enjoy the natural phenomena from a harbour cruise at Lerwick in the *Dim Riv*, a 40-foot replica of a Norse longship.

Tourism in 1990/91 brought in about £8 million to the Shetland Islands. Sheep rearing is an important part of Shetland life and the famous knitwear is now the basis for an important industry and boost to the tourist trade. The RSPB nature reserve at Loch Spiggie has puffin, arctic tern, curlew, oyster catchers and gannet, the largest of the islands' birds.

Jarlshof prehistoric site at Sumburgh spans 3000 years of life on Mainland and the 43-foot broch, or tower, of Mousa, an island which is only 15 minutes from Mainland, is also of interest. The Shetland Museum at Lerwick is a centre for local archaeology, folk life and salvaged items from famous shipwrecks. The Crofthouse Museum at Voe, Dunrossness is part of the main museum and it shows the furniture and fittings of a genuine 1870s croft house in a realistic setting. Picturesque Scalloway, once the capital of the islands, has Scandinavian-type houses and a medieval castle

and nearby Tingwall Loch was the site of the Norse Parliament, or Ting. Modern day interest is to be found at Sullom Voe, the site of the largest oil terminal in Europe.

Diagram 12.2   Summary map of the highlands and islands of Scotland

◇ Summary of attractions ◇

For children

Perth Leisure Pool, Tayside
Loch Ness Monster Exhibition,
    Drumnadrochit, Highland
Storybook Glen, Maryculter, near Aberdeen
West Highland steam train
Strathspey steam railway, Highland
Dim Riv longship, Lerwick

Conservation areas

AONB and Forest Parks
Loch Lomond, Central
Loch Ness, Highland
The Trossachs, Central
Cairngorms, Highland
Blairdrummond Safari Park, Central
Aviemore, Highland
Aden Country Park, Mintlaw, Grampian
Glenmore Forest Park, Aviemore, Highland
Haddo Country Park, Ellon, Grampian
Ben Nevis, near Fort William, Highland
Inverewe Gardens, Gairloch, Highland
RSPB, Loch Spiggie, Shetland

Historical heritage

Aberdeen Art Gallery
Stirling Castle
Regimental Museum, Stirling, Central
Inverness Museum and Art Gallery
Urquhart Castle, Drumnadrochit, Loch Ness,
    Highland
Blair Castle, Pitlochry, Tayside
Glencoe Visitor Centre, near Fort William,
    Highland
Culloden Moor Visitor Centre, near Inverness,
    Highland
Highland Folk Museum, Kingussie, Highland
Tain and District Museum, Highland

Balmoral Castle, Grampian
Glamis Castle, Tayside
Clan Donald Centre, Skye
Standing Stones, Lewis
Black House Museum, Arnol, Lewis
Skara Brae, Orkney
Tankerness House, Orkney
Jarlshof, Shetland
Shetland Museum, Lerwick

Traditional and industrial heritage

Glenturret Distillery, Crieff, Tayside
Harris tweed garments
Baxter's, Fochabers, Highland
Shetland knitwear
Glenfiddich Distillery, Highland
Stuart Strathearn Crystal, Crieff, Tayside
West Highland steam train
Strathspey steam railway
Sullom Voe Oil Terminal, Shetland

Local events and festivals

January	Up Helly Aa Fire Festival, Lerwick
March	Perthshire Musical Festival
April	Shetland Folk Festival
May	Perth Festival of the Arts
	Atholl Highlanders Parade, Blair Castle, Tayside
May to September	over 70 Highland Gatherings
August	Perth Agricultral Show
September	Aviemore Whisky Festival
	Braemar Gathering
	Ben Nevis Race, Fort William
October	World Piping Championships, Blair Atholl
31 December	Flambeaux Procession, Comrie, Tayside

13 *North Wales*

The North Wales Regional Council area covers the counties of:

- **Clywd**
- **Gwynedd**
- **the island of Anglesey.**

The area is very popular with visitors from the north west of England from where access by road is very easy via the fast A55 dual carriageway. Access is also reasonably easy from other parts of the country via the M6, M54 and A5. There are no airports in North Wales but the area is served by the airports at Liverpool and Manchester. Holyhead on Anglesey is the entry port for many visitors from Ireland and British Rail connections to that port from London, via Crewe and Chester, serve the entire northern coast of Wales.

In 1989, Wales attracted about the same number of UK visitors as Scotland. However, Wales attracted only half the number of overseas visitors. In that year Wales had a 25 per cent increase in the number of visits to wildlife attractions, and this was only surpassed in the UK by the number of such visits in Yorkshire and Humberside. The increase in the number of visits to wildlife attractions was put down to better marketing, extra facilities being provided and more favourable weather. Wales also had the greatest increase in the number of children visiting wildlife attractions in 1989 and this could indicate an improvement in children's facilities. Abbey Farm Museum at Holywell reached its capacity on more than one occasion and both the Anglesey Sea Zoo and the Welsh Mountain Zoo at Colwyn Bay had about 200 000 visitors in 1989.

We shall consider the attractions of North Wales under the headings of:

- natural attractions of Snowdonia National Park, Areas of Outstanding Natural Beauty (AONB) and country parks
- historical attractions from castles to stately homes
- industrial attractions from slate mines to woollen mills
- family entertainment in traditional seaside resorts.

Natural attractions

Snowdonia National Park covers 840 square miles of beautiful scenery from mountains to coastline. The Park stretches from Conwy in the north to Aberdyfi in the south, and from Bala in the east to Harlech on the west coast. Established in 1951, the Park is administered by Gwynedd County Council but most of the land in the National Park is privately owned, with access by public footpaths. Many footpaths have been eroded and widened by over 10 million visitors a year and, in the 1980s, the Snowdon Management Scheme, supported by the Countryside Commission, drained paths and repaired serious erosion on Mount Snowdon, at the same time publicising guidelines for visitors.

By...PREVENTING FURTHER EROSION

In some places the footpaths have been eroded to more than 40 feet wide and several feet deep. The summit is especially badly eroded. Erosion is ugly and can be dangerous. Please keep to the footpath to prevent further erosion.

RESPECTING PRIVATE LAND AND STOCK

Did you know that nearly all of Snowdon is privately owned by farmers and used for sheep grazing? Indeed, sheep farming on Snowdon supports more than 20 farmers and their families. Please keep dogs on a lead. Do not climb or damage stone walls and fences - they are vital to efficient farm management.

Remember:- You are on a footpath passing through private property. Please also remember that not all footpaths on Snowdon are public.

TOLERATING THE REPAIR WORK IN PROGRESS

21 Estate Workers are working to drain the paths and to repair the serious erosion damage. Using local natural materials, the aim is to improve the footpaths so that walkers are not tempted to stray from them. Volunteer work gangs are also helping. The work is hard and the weather is often bad.

RESPECTING WILDLIFE

Much of Snowdon has been made into a National Nature Reserve. This is because there are many very rare plants growing on the mountain. Some of these plants are found only on Snowdon. Please keep to the footpaths to avoid trampling these rare plants. Do not pick them.

TAKING YOUR LITTER HOME

Litter is unsightly and often causes injury to livestock — tins and glass can lame and polythene bags can suffocate. If you have the energy to carry full tins and bottles up the mountain, why not carry them back down when they are empty? *Take your litter home with you.*

ASKING NATIONAL PARK FIELD STAFF

As part of the Snowdon Management Scheme, extra Wardens and Information Staff are present on and around the mountain to give advice to walkers. They will be pleased to help you.

AVOIDING TRAFFIC PROBLEMS

Please use the car parks around the mountain. Do not park illegally on clearways or block farm or field accesses. There is a large car park at Nant Peris if Pen-y-Pass is full.

VOLUNTEERING YOUR SERVICES

The job of repairing the footpaths is an enormous one. We have tools and accommodation facilities for Volunteer Groups. We need all the help we can get.

If you wish to know more about the Snowdon Management Scheme or wish to help in some way, please contact Rod Gritten, Snowdonia National Park Offices, Penrhyndeudraeth, Gwynedd LL48 6LF. Tel: Penrhyndeudraeth (0766) 770274

0766 770274

Guidelines for walkers in Snowdonia National Park entitled How can you protect the National Park?

◇ **Activity:** *Case study* ◇

Page 85 shows one of the leaflets used to alert the public to the erosion problems faced by Snowdonia National Park. Read the advice given and if possible make a visit to a local National Park or AONB.

1 What are the problems faced by your chosen area with regard to public use?
2 If left unsupervised, what potential problems could develop in your chosen area?
3 Design three leaflets to encourage the public to take more care of the natural environment in your chosen area. These leaflets should be targeted at:
   • children under the age of 12
   • young people aged 16–18
   • parents of young children.

National Parks have a dual role of preserving the countryside and providing facilities for quiet recreation. Within Snowdonia National Park there are ample facilities for:

◆ walking	◆ climbing
◆ sailing	◆ canoeing
◆ hill walking	◆ pony trekking
◆ surfboarding	◆ fishing.

Visitor centres throughout the Park provide bed-booking systems and information about nature reserves, sites of scientific interest and guided walks. National Park Wardens, who can be easily identified in their distinctive red and blue uniforms or by their white vehicles, assist both visitors and residents in the Park.

The summit of Snowdon can be approached from each side and five paths are clearly marked, namely:

• the Rhyd ddu path
• the Llanberis path
• the Miners' track
• the Watkin path
• the Snowdon Ranger.

The Snowdon Sherpa bus, which follows a circular route, enables visitors to park their cars outside the main area, with the knowledge that they can take the bus at the beginning and end of their walk. The

mountain railway from Llanberis takes visitors to the top the easy way. The upper terminus is just below the summit at 3494 feet and the trains cover the 4.6 miles in approximately an hour. A spectacular way of seeing the summit is from the pleasure flights which operate from the Caernarfon Air Museum in a genuine 'thirties' de Havilland Rapide bi-plane.

Betws-y-Coed, a compact picturesque town, set in the Gwydyr forest at the foot of Snowdon, caters for the needs of walkers and climbers. This inland resort, which has been popular since Victorian times, has one of the largest Tourist Information Centres in the area and excellent accommodation and shops. Three rivers meet in the town at the Swallow Falls, a popular place for picnics and relaxation.

Bala also caters for visitors to the Park, especially to Llyn Tegid or Lake Bala, the largest natural lake in Wales. The lake is famous for its fishing and variety of boating and sailing. The exceptionally wide main street of Bala has an abundance of shops and restaurants.

Beddgelert, a pretty village to the south of Snowdon markets itself as the 'heart of Snowdonia'. The setting of the village in the fields, trees, rivers and lakes of the Gwynant valley, is beautiful against the backdrop of Mount Snowdon. There is a wide range of both accommodation and activities in the area.

South of Snowdonia, the Lleyn peninsula with its gentle landscape and over 100 miles of coastline, has been designated as an AONB. The main resorts along the coast are described later in the chapter, but yachting, windsurfing, water skiing, golf courses and pony trekking are all available and, within an hour's drive, tourists can walk and climb in the National Park.

The Forestry Commission protects areas around Aberystwyth, to the south of Bala and in the Llangollen area, as well as the forest around Betws-y-Coed, which forms an integral part of the National Park. The forests around Llangollen are only 40 miles from Merseyside but the Victorian inland resort is a haven of peace. As well as enjoying the natural surroundings, visitors to Llangollen can ride on a unique horse-drawn canal barge or have a meal aboard a steam train on a 3-hour evening trip or step back in time in a

Victorian schoolroom. Llangollen is also the venue for the International Musical Eisteddfod in July each year, when singers and dancers congregate from all over the world for a very colourful fortnight. Loggerheads Country Park, 3 miles outside Mold to the north of Llangollen, is a beautiful setting for gentle walks and panoramic views across the River Dee.

The Welsh Mountain Zoo and Gardens at Colwyn Bay is in a fantastic setting overlooking Snowdonia, Anglesey and the North Wales coastline. Animals in the zoo include elephants, lions, bears, deer and penguins, and a tarzan trail provides entertainment for young children. The zoo's education unit helps local schools in their programmes with regard to wildlife conservation.

Bodnant Garden, also at Colwyn Bay, is one of the finest gardens in Britain. Set in 100 acres it is especially beautiful in the spring with an abundance of rhododendrons, roses, camellias and magnolias. The backdrop of Snowdon and views of Colwyn Bay both add to the attractive setting of the garden.

Historical attractions

The royal castles of North Wales, built by Edward I in the thirteenth century are listed as World Heritage Sites by UNESCO. These castles include:

- Flint
- Conwy
- Caernarfon
- Aberystwyth
- Rhuddlan
- Beaumaris
- Harlech
- Builth.

Rhuddlan Castle, which stood on the coast before the bay silted up, is now a ruin overlooking the Vale of Clwyd. Conwy Castle is beautifully preserved and its fortress towers and the walls of the old city look very picturesque to visitors who cross the River Conwy on the modern bridge at the end of the A55. Caernarfon Castle is famous as the setting for the investiture of Prince Charles as Prince of Wales in 1969, and Harlech, further south, has commanding views over the dunelands and estuaries of Cardigan and Tremadog Bays. Dating from the same period as the castles, the Valle Crucis Abbey, west of Llangollen, is a lovely ruin of a Cistercian abbey. An exhibition portrays

the lives of the monks at that time and today's visitors can savour the quiet peaceful surroundings.

The National Trust has several properties in North Wales, among them Chirk Castle, Penrhyn Castle and Erddig. Chirk Castle, near Wrexham, has some elaborate Robert Adam plasterwork in its staterooms and a beautiful eighteenth-century garden. Penrhyn Castle is a fantasy castle, built between 1820 and 1840 in the style of the twelfth century. Many of the staterooms retain their original decoration and the upstairs rooms command superb views of the mountains of the National Park and the Menai Strait. Erddig, also near Wrexham, was built in the seventeenth century and is described by the National Trust as 'the most evocative upstairs–downstairs house in Britain'. The Country Park surrounding the house is well laid out with walks for visitors and an information centre.

Industrial heritage

Slate quarries were for centuries an important source of employment in North Wales, with the Dinorwic Quarry at Llanberis alone employing 3000 people at its peak of production about 1900. The Welsh Slate Museum is housed in the former Dinorwic Quarry workshops in Gilfach Ddu, where exhibits include the largest waterwheel in Wales and a steam locomotive and rolling stock. The Llanberis Lake Railway runs from the car park along the shores of Llyn Padarn. The Padarn Country Park also has watersports on the lake, a collection of surgical equipment in the former Quarry Hospital and various craft shops and displays relating to the social history of the area.

Blaenau Ffestiniog at the foot of Mount Snowdon is regarded as the slate capital of the world. The Llechwedd Slate Caverns, the Inigo Jones Slate Works and the Gloddfa Ganol Slate Mine are all open to the public. In the Llechwedd Slate Caverns visitors can take two rides underground to see the miners' passageways, spectacular underground caverns, so unusual that they were used in a Walt Disney film, and tableaux illustrating mining techniques. Above the surface the miners' village has been restored and visitors can change money in the Old Bank to spend pre-decimalisation coins in the shops and pub. The Inigo Jones Slate Works at Groeslon near Caernarfon is a working concern where visitors can watch the processes of cutting, polishing and engraving slate clocks, lamps, chess sets, name plates and fireplaces. Visitors can try engraving slate for themselves and souvenirs can be purchased in the showroom. Gloddfa Ganol, in Blaenau Ffestiniog, is a working mine but special conducted tours can be arranged into the mine and all visitors can take the quarrymen's train to the main mine entrance. Quarrymen can be observed sawing and splitting the slate, and the museum and audiovisual presentation help visitors to appreciate the complexity of the slate industry.

In their heyday most mines had steam railways to transport the slate and many of these little railways have survived to this day, although their use nowadays is mainly to transport tourists. The most famous of these railways is probably the Ffestiniog Railway which runs in the season from Porthmadog to Blaenau Ffestiniog, past lakes and waterfalls up the side of Snowdon. The journey takes visitors the 13.5 miles to 700 feet above sea level in just over an hour. Tourists can buy a Narrow Gauge Wanderer Ticket which gives them unlimited travel for four or eight days on the following railways in Wales:

♦ Ffestiniog	♦ Talyllyn
♦ Vale of Rheidol	♦ Bala Lake
♦ Welshpool and Llanfair	♦ Llanberis Lake
♦ West Highland	♦ Brecon Mountain.

Bersham Industrial Heritage Centre just south of Wrexham is the site of an eighteenth-century ironworks. Worksheets and teachers' resources make this a popular choice for school visits. The exhibits include the original pumping engine, remains of the ironworks, miners' tools, photographs and displays. The 8-mile Clywedog Trail takes visitors through sites in the area connected with lead and coal mining, iron and paper manufacturing as well as agriculture.

Weaving has also been an important industry in Wales for many centuries. Many mills were sited next to streams where the rough wool could be washed in soft water and the stream could be used to power the waterwheel of the mill. Penmachno Woollen Mill, south of Betws-y-Coed and Trefriw Woollen Mills, near Llanrwst are open to the public. In both mills visitors can see the various stages of producing woollen goods, and their shops sell knitwear, tweeds and bedspreads, as well as traditional wooden lovespoons such as shepherds and weavers made for their sweethearts long ago.

Tourism itself is a long-established industry in North Wales as shown by the construction in 1902 of the Great Orme Tramway at Llandudno with the express purpose of taking tourists up the Great Orme. This is the only cable hauled tramway in Britain. The first part of the journey climbs steeply through old terraced streets and then passengers disembark and take the second part of the journey in a cable lift car through the Great Orme Country Park to the summit at 679 feet above sea level. On a good day the views over Llandudno Bay are tremendous.

Modern tourists have shopping high on their list of pleasures and North Wales caters well for this with a variety of craft shops. Ruthin Craft Centre is a purpose built complex of 14 units in the former railway station and goods yard. Tyn Llan Crafts, just five minutes from Porthmadog is housed in a range of old farm buildings. Specialist craft shops throughout the area also include walking sticks at Croesor, Penrhyndeudraeth, outdoor wall-decorations of butterflies at Llangollen and pottery at Dolwyddlan and Llanberis.

Family entertainment and seaside resorts

The north coast of Wales and the Lleyn peninsula are firm favourites with families. The main north coast resorts are Prestatyn, Rhyl, Colwyn Bay, and Llandudno.

♦ Prestatyn is a quiet resort clustered around its white sandy beach. Much of the local accommodation is in the caravan parks between the main coastal road and the beach. Pontins have their largest holiday camp right on the beach at the far end of the town. The Nova is a modern swimming and entertainment complex aimed at families, and the small resort also has more traditional entertainment such as putting greens, boating pools and go-karts.

♦ Rhyl, a much larger resort to the west of

Prestatyn is renowned as a sun spot. However, if the weather fails, the Rhyl Suncentre has indoor tropically heated splash pools, slides and a wave pool. Shopping and sports facilities are excellent and there is a variety of accommodation in the town. Ocean Beach Amusements is a traditional fun fair with white knuckle rides and novelties for children.

- Colwyn Bay is a quieter resort with a 3-mile crescent-shaped promenade. The pedestrianised shopping area is popular and the Welsh Mountain Zoo is a favourite with children. Eirias Park gives commanding views of the promenade and beach and Dinosaur World within the park has lifesize models.

- Llandudno is the largest resort in North Wales and its hotels and shops reflect its Victorian origins. The resort nestles between the two headlands of the Great and Little Orme and its attractions include the pier, two beautiful beaches, boat trips, a dry ski slope and the tramway and cable lift described above. The Rabbit Hole is an unusual re-creation of the little world of Alice in Wonderland where visitors can wander through tableaux from the book with their own personal stereo commentary. The original Alice Liddell, for whom Lewis Carroll wrote the book, spent her summer holidays at Penmorfa, the family residence in Llandudno. There is a wide variety of accommodation in the resort, much of it fronting onto Llandudno Bay.

Travelling around the coast, the castle towns of Conwy and Caernarfon are popular with tourists and day trippers alike and can be very busy in the summer. Conwy boasts the smallest house in Britain, which has just one room upstairs and one downstairs. The house is so small that, when closed, the trap door above the ladder to the second floor is the only real floor space in the bedroom.

The Lleyn peninsular has quieter resorts than the north coast including Abersoch, Pwllheli, Criccieth and Porthmadog.

- Abersoch at the tip of the peninsula has some beautifully restored cottages and sleek vessels lie at anchor in the harbour. The area is popular for second homes and caravan parks.

- Pwllheli is a quiet town which comes alive on market day. The shops are small, but unusual for tourists from cities, and the harbour has some lovely views of Tremadog Bay.

- Criccieth is a hilly fishing village with two bays on either side of the headland. The ruins of the castle make a picturesque sight on top of the headland. The castle was built before the arrival of Edward I who strengthened it to form one of his fortresses.

- Porthmadog is the busiest of the Lleyn peninsula resorts. The approach from the east is via an extremely narrow toll road built in the early 1800s across the bay. Traffic stopping to pay the token toll and modern coaches and lorries which prove to be too wide for access both contribute to making this one of the main bottlenecks for traffic in North Wales. The Ffestiniog Railway runs from the town and just beyond its station is the fantasy 'town' of Portmeirion. Created by the architect Sir Clough Williams-Ellis, this little village of Italian style buildings clings to the cliff side. Exotic plants flourish in the mild climate and all the cottages and houses are let as holiday accommodation. Visitors pay an admission fee and in 1989 the village attracted over 300 000 people. Portmeirion's fame has spread far beyond North Wales through the popularity of its famous colourful pottery.

Anglesey

The Isle of Anglesey can be reached by either of two bridges across the Menai Strait. On both bridges, visitors are greeted with a sign saying *Môn Mâm Cymru* which means 'Anglesey, Mother of Wales'. The island is very fertile and has traditionally supplied agricultural produce for the more mountainous mainland. The green fields and wooded shores are very popular with tourists and much of the 125 miles of coastline has been designated as either AONB or Heritage Coastlines. There are beautiful beaches all around the island from the 15 square miles of white sand at *Traeth Coch* or 'Red Wharf Bay' to rocky inlets such as Porth Trwyn in the north, which is popular for swimming.

To the west of Holyhead, the port from which boats go to Ireland, is the South Stack Lighthouse. It is at the South Stack that the RSPB have a reserve with puffins, ravens, chuffs and guillemots.

Throughout Wales many place names begin with the prefix *Llan* which means a clearing, a plot of consecrated land or possibly a church. Llan is generally followed by the name of the local saint, so Llanfair means church of Mary. As there are several places beginning with Llanfair, a local name was sometimes added. It is in this way that Llanfair Pwllgwyngyll was named, but this was lengthened even more in the nineteenth century, as a hoax on tourists, to

LLANFAIRPWLLGWYNGYLLGOGERYCHWYRN -
DROBWLLLLANTYSILIOGOGOGOCH.

Hoax or not, the name still draws tourists and nowadays the railway station is the premises of James Pringle Weavers where tourists can buy genuine Welsh knitwear at factory prices.

Anglesey continues to attract tourists with leisure centres at Holyhead, Plas Arthur and Amlwch and the Anglesey Sea Zoo at Brynsiencyn. The Sea Zoo, which is entirely undercover, allows visitors to see a great variety of fish, walk through a shipwreck and watch the ebb and flow of the tides in a special 'tide tank'.

The island also has historical interest with Edward I's largest castle at Beaumaris and, in the same town, the Museum of Childhood and a Victorian Gaol. The National Trust maintains Plas Newydd, the beautiful eighteenth-century former home of James Wyatt. The interior has memorable paintings and furniture and the grounds have landscaped gardens, an adventure playground for children and uninterrupted views across the Menai Strait. Hen Blas is a seventeenth-century manor house but the entire estate has been developed with tourists in mind. There are landscaped gardens, a working smithy, shire horse cart rides, a golf driving range and falconry displays.

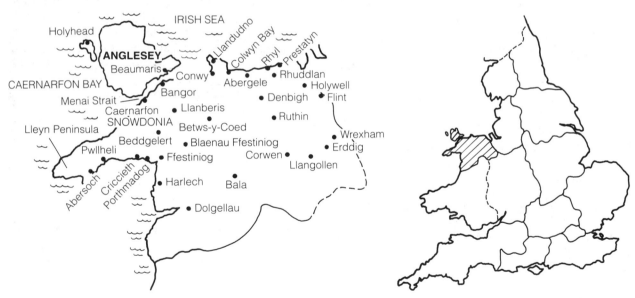

Diagram 13.1   Summary map of North Wales

◇ **Summary of attractions** ◇

Seaside resorts

Abersoch, Gwynedd
Pwllheli, Gwynedd
Porthmadog, Gwynedd
Criccieth, Gwynedd
Llandudno, Gwynedd
Prestatyn, Clwyd
Rhyl, Clwyd
Colwyn Bay, Clwyd

Inland resorts

Betws-y-Coed, Gwynedd
Llangollen, Gwynedd
Bala, Gwynedd
Beddgelert, Gwynedd

Conservation areas

Snowdonia National Park
Loggerheads Country Park, Clwyd
Lake Bala, Gwynedd
Bodnant Gardens, Colwyn Bay, Clwyd
Lleyn peninsula, Gwynedd
Erddig Country Park, Gwynedd
Great Orme Country Park, Gwynedd
Padarn Country Park
South Stack RSPB Bird Sanctuary, Anglesey
AONB and Heritage Coasts of Anglesey

Family attractions

Caernarfon Air Museum, Gwynedd
Welsh Mountain Zoo, Colwyn Bay, Clwyd
The Rabbit Hole, Llandudno, Gwynedd
Portmeirion, near Portmadog, Gwynedd
Anglesey Sea Zoo
Rhyl Suncentre, Clwyd

Historical heritage

Royal castles in
  Flint, Clwyd
  Rhuddlan, Clwyd
  Conwy, Gwynedd
  Beaumaris, Anglesey
  Caernarfon, Gwynedd
  Harlech, Gwynedd
  Aberystwyth, Dyfed
  Builth, Powys
Valle Crucis Abbey, Llangollen, Clwyd
Chirk Castle, Wrexham, Clwyd
Penrhyn Castle, Bangor, Gwynedd
Erddig, Wrexham, Clwyd
Plas Newydd, Anglesey
Hen Blas, Anglesey

Industrial heritage

Welsh Slate Museum, Llanberis, Gwynedd
Llechwedd Slate Caverns, Blaenau Ffestiniog,
  Gwynedd
Inigo Jones Slate Works, Gwynedd
Gloddfa Ganol Slate Mine, Blaenau Ffestiniog,
  Gwynedd
Bersham Industrial Heritage Centre,
  Wrexham, Clwyd
Clywedog Trail, Wrexham, Clwyd
Penmachno Woollen Mills, Gwynedd
Trefriw Woollen Mills, Gwynedd
Ruthin Craft Centre, Clwyd
Tyn Llan Craft Centre, Gwynedd
Piggery Pottery, Llanberis
The Butterfly Man, Corwen, Clwyd

Steam railways at
Ffestiniog, Gwynedd
Talyllyn, Gwynedd
Vale of Rheidol, Dyfed
Bala Lake, Gwynedd
Welshpool and Llanfair, Powys
Llanberis Lake, Gwynedd
West Highland, Gwynedd

Local events and festivals

May	International Jazz Festival, Llangollen
	Beaumaris Festival, Anglesey
June	Criccieth Music Festival
	North Wales Antique Fair, Bodelwyddan Castle, near Abergele
July	The Snowdon Race
	Menai Strait Regatta Fortnight
	International Musical Eisteddfod, Llangollen
August	Anglesey Agricultural Show
October	Menai Bridge Fair
November	Wild Water Canoeing Race, Llangollen
	Holyhead Arts Festival

14 *South Wales*

In this chapter we shall consider the counties of:

- **Dyfed**
- **Powys**
- **Gwent**
- **West Glamorgan**
- **Mid Glamorgan**
- **South Glamorgan.**

These counties are marketed by the Mid Wales and the South Wales Tourist Councils, and the south west corner of Dyfed also markets itself under its previous county name of Pembrokeshire.

By road, London is less than 3 hours from South Wales via the M4 and then the A40 out to Haverfordwest, and the A487 takes motorists right up the west coast of Wales. British Rail links from Fishguard to Bristol, and to the north west through Hereford and Crewe mean that the area is easily accessible from all parts of Britain. A cross country route from Swansea to Shrewsbury makes inland resorts and scenery equally accessible. Ferries operate a 3.5-hour service throughout the year from Fishguard to Rosslare in the Republic of Ireland, and there is a 10-hour seasonal service from Swansea to Cork. Cardiff, the capital of Wales, has an international airport.

Tourism in South Wales is centred mainly on the natural attractions of the mountains and coast, and on the industrial mining heritage of the region. In 1983 the last of the mines in the Rhondda Valley closed and the opportunity was taken to launch a major tourism, recreational and heritage project. The local authorities, the Welsh Development Agency and the Wales Tourist Board put forward a plan to landscape tip sites and attract visitors

into the area, thus creating new jobs and enhancing the environment, with new facilities for local people. The development plan spans 4 years from 1990 to 1993. In its first year the Park received 18 618 visitors, and that was even before the major attraction at the restored pit head buildings opened. The completed Rhondda Heritage Park will have an underground experience, a 1920s mining village, a modern reception and exhibition area, accommodation, and footpaths and mountain top viewpoints planned by the Forestry Commission.

We shall study the attractions of South Wales under the headings of:

- natural attractions, from coastline to mountains
- family entertainment in seaside and inland resorts
- historical attractions of castles, stately homes and museums
- industrial heritage of silver, gold and coal mining, the maritime heritage of Swansea and Cardiff and new technological developments.

...tractions

...tionally famous for its castles and ...epresented in South Wales from the ...r castle at Chepstow to the Victorian ...nts of Cardiff Castle.

...w Castle is in a superb setting above the ...Wye guarding the border between ...d and Wales. It was probably the first ...castle in Britain but was improved and ...d to right up to the Civil War making it ...resting from an architectural point of view. ...broke Castle in Dyfed was first built by the ...rmans but was completely rebuilt in the ...iddle Ages. It is famous as the birthplace of ...he first Tudor King and also as the site of a 7-week seige led by Cromwell during the Civil War.

- Caerphilly Castle in Mid Glamorgan and Manorbier Castle in Dyfed both date from the thirteenth century, as can be seen from their massive battlements and towers. Caerphilly is famous for the fact that one of its towers leans at an angle that would rival the Leaning Tower of Pisa, and Manorbier is beautifully located in the Pembrokeshire Coast National Park.
- Caldicot Castle in Gwent retains much of its fourteenth-century grandeur, in spite of being extensively modernised in the last century. It is popular nowadays for its museum, country park and regular medieval banquets.
- Cardiff Castle in South Glamorgan has Roman, Norman and Victorian connections. The Norman motte and keep are one of the best preserved in Europe but they contrast sharply with Victorian renovations, such as the fantasy octagonal tower.

Many of the Welsh castles are in the care of CADW, the Heritage Monuments section of the Welsh Office. This is comparable to English Heritage in England and similar entrance concessions apply to those who join CADW as to those who join English Heritage. An additional bonus for members of either organisation is that they receive free entry to properties in both England and Wales in their second and subsequent years of membership.

Penhow Castle in Gwent is Wales' oldest inhabited castle and was originally a small border fortress. Nowadays it presents a picture of life over seven centuries from the twelfth-century Great Hall to a Victorian housekeeper's room. Welsh country farmhouse feasts are provided in the tithe barn and the Visitor Centre has its own inn, the Castle Arms. Tredegar House, also in Gwent is South Wales' finest country house. Set in 90 acres of parkland, the seventeenth-century house has over 40 beautifully refurbished rooms. Carriage rides, self-guided trails, craft workshops, boating and an adventure playground all contribute to a full day's entertainment.

Powis Castle in Welshpool receives over 100 000 visitors each year. The castle was built in the thirteenth century but its country house collection includes Georgian furniture, tapestries and pictures. Many of the treasures were inherited from Clive of India, whose son married a Powis heiress.

The National Museum of Wales' main building is located in Cardiff where the collection includes paintings, silver, ceramics and archaeological artefacts. A wealth of local culture is displayed in the Welsh Folk Museum at St Fagans outside Cardiff. The old farmhouses, cottages, tannery, school and chapel of the outdoor museum were visited in 1990 by 264 897 people. The Newport Museum and Art Gallery received over 130 000 visitors in 1990, possibly drawn by the specialist displays which relate to local connections with the Chartist Movement of 1838–40.

More recent, innovative museums in South Wales include the Castle Hill Museum of the Home in Pembroke which received the Prince of Wales Award in the first year it was opened. Over 3000 artefacts related to everyday life in Wales are displayed in a domestic setting. The WH Smith 1920s shop replica in Newtown in Powys has been completely restored in its original state and is an unusual combination of museum and shop. A more recent attraction is the Llancaiach Fawr Manor in Nelson, Mid Glamorgan, where life during the era of the Civil War is brought vividly to life through events and banquets.

Industrial heritage

The mining heritage of Wales is remembered in silver, gold and coal mines which are open to the

Natural attractions

Two of the 11 National Parks of England and Wales are in this area, namely the Brecon Beacons National Park and the Pembrokeshire Coast National Park. The Brecon Beacons has open moorland, gentle pastures and lonely mountain summits, and the Park's limestone cliffs have interesting caves, hidden streams and some of the most spectacular waterfalls in the British Isles. The Dan-Yr-Ogof Showcaves at Abercraf, midway between Brecon and Swansea, have received nine tourism awards in recent years. In 1990 the caves welcomed 200 000 visitors to see the Cathedral Showcave, the largest single chamber of any British showcave, and the Bone Cave which was inhabited by humans 3000 years ago. The Brecon Mountain Railway's 1-hour trip covers 4 miles of beautiful scenery along the side of the Taf Fechan Reservoir, and the Brecon Beacons Mountain Centre at Libanus receives over 100 000 visitors each year.

The Pembrokeshire Coast National Park covers 180 miles of coastline, from St Dogmaels near Cardigan to Amroth near Tenby. The Park has islands, sand dunes and impressive cliffs, with associated bird life. Two of the islands hold the largest breeding colonies of puffins in southern Britain. Skokholm holds about 2500 pairs of puffins, and Skomer has an even larger colony with 6000. In both National Parks there is a Ranger Service which provides facilities such as guided walks for all abilities, and discovery days, for a variety of interests.

There are also two designated Areas of Outstanding Natural Beauty (AONB) in South Wales, namely the Wye Valley and the Gower Peninsula. Chepstow and Monmouth are both ideal centres for holidays in the Wye Valley. Tintern Abbey, which is located halfway between the two towns, epitomises the beauty of this area with its splendid peaceful scenery of green wooded slopes in the summer and golden tints in the autumn. The Gower Peninsula, to the west of

Pembrokeshire Coast National Park

Swansea, is a haven of tranquillity where the sea is never far away and rocky headlands, such as the Mumbles, often hide tiny sandy beaches which were once the haunt of smugglers.

Offa's Dyke is one of the most famous Long Distance Trails in the UK. It follows the route of the boundary dyke built by Offa, King of Mercia in the eighth century. Starting at the Sedbury Cliffs south of Chepstow in Gwent, it covers 168 miles to the River Dee in Clwyd. There is an Offa's Dyke Information and Heritage Centre at Knighton in Powys which has a range of publications, library, slide shows and exhibitions related to walking in the area.

In an area renowned for its beauty it is not surprising to find several Country Parks. These include:

- Cosmeston Lakes Country Park in South Glamorgan, which covers over 200 acres of lakes, woodland and meadows. The park was formerly a limestone quarry but was landscaped and developed as a leisure centre during the 1980s. A unique feature of the park is its medieval village which has been excavated and reconstructed on its original site.
- Margam Park near Port Talbot in West Glamorgan received over 250 000 visitors in 1990. The park covers 800 acres within which are the impressive castle, an adventure playground, a miniature nursery rhyme village, one of Europe's largest mazes, orangery gardens, putting and giant chess. A programme of events throughout the year ensures a variety of entertainment, from craft fairs to military displays.
- Afan Argoed Country Park, also near Port Talbot, is set in a beautiful deep sided forested valley which is known locally as 'little Switzerland'. Countryside and forestry walks are well signposted and a cycle hire centre helps visitors make full use of a 14-mile cycle way. Within the park is the Welsh Miners Museum which we shall consider later in this chapter.

Cwmcarn Forest Drive is a 7-mile scenic route, which was developed by the Forestry Commission for motorists through Gwent. The route offers spectacular views over the Bristol Channel, and a number of picnic sites with play areas, barbecues and forest walks have been provided.

Wildlife Parks are popular in South Wales. The most frequently visited in 1990 was Penscynor Wildlife Park at Cilfrew in West Glamorgan, which received over 280 000 visitors. Animals in the park include chimpanzees, monkeys, penguins and tropical birds. Play areas, a chairlift and an alpine slide all contribute to enjoyment for a family day out. Manor House Wildlife and Leisure Park at St Florence, near Tenby, in Dyfed received over 100 000 visitors in 1990. Falconry is a special attraction at this park, as well as an animal and bird collection, attractive gardens and a model railway. The Welsh Hawking Centre at Barry in South Glamorgan has over 200 birds of prey, including eagles, owls, buzzards, hawks and falcons.

◇ **Activity:** *Countryside walking tour* ◇

In such a beautiful area as South Wales there could be another Long Distance Trail. Consider the natural attractions of the area and consult the terrain, using an Ordnance Survey Map.

Choose a specific area of at least 400 square miles or 1000 square kilometres and design a countryside route which could be walked in about a week. Break the walk into sections which can be covered in a day, and consider places for overnight stops.

Summarise your walking tour on an illustrated map which indicates:

- distance
- terrain
- particular natural attractions
- other attractions
- main accommodation points for overnight stops.

Resorts and family entertainment

Many seaside resorts in South Wales are as yet unspoilt by commercialisation and certainly none could be regarded as meccas of loud entertainment. Along the south coast, west of Cardiff, we shall consider Porthcawl, Saundersfoot and Tenby, and moving up the west coast, north of Cardigan, we shall look at New Quay and Aberystwyth.

- Porthcawl has two south facing beaches at Sandy Bay and Trecco Bay. The Coney Beach amusement complex, waterslides and splash pool are open all day and a range of entertainment is provided in the evening at the Grand Pavilion on the Esplanade. Either side of the resort is the solitude of sand dunes and only 5 miles away at Ogmore is the start of the Glamorgan Heritage Coast where the cliffs have been eroded by the sea into strange, spectacular shapes.
- Saundersfoot developed as a resort from an eighteenth-century fishing village and coal port. The resort's history gives it some original features such as a Barbecue Restaurant which was originally the colliery offices. The 3 miles of sandy beach are backed by shops, a peaceful park and cliff walks. Fresh fish is landed at the harbour each day, and boats can be chartered by more adventurous visitors.
- Tenby is Saundersfoot's brasher neighbour, which offers everything one would expect in a modern holiday resort. The town has four beaches and a picturesque harbour. The winding alleys of the small medieval town add to the enjoyment of a family holiday.
- New Quay is a picturesque fishing village with terraced cottages clinging to its steep cliffs which descend sharply to the beach and harbour. Dylan Thomas lived near New Quay and he is said to have referred to the resort in *Under Milk Wood* as the 'cliff-perched town at the far end of Wales'. The high cliffs afford visitors spectacular views of Cardigan Bay.
- Aberystwyth is the largest town and principal shopping centre of Mid Wales, as well as being an ideal centre for touring the region. At the northern end of the promenade is the longest electric cliff railway in Britain, and, in the summer, the Vale of Rheidol narrow gauge steam railway takes visitors 680 feet up the hillside along the 12-mile track. As well as being a popular holiday destination, Aberystwyth has the National Library of Wales and the Ceredigion Museum, which is housed in a restored music hall.

We have seen that natural attractions in South

Wales in
coast
re

Historical a

Wales is inter
these are well
ancient bord
embellishm

P
nin
town
and h
architectu
Festival, sh
and hotel sta
are banned fro
by horses and ca
sea level, Llandri
some of the most be
and is an ideal touring

- Chepst
River
Engla
ston
add
inte
- Pe
- N

Visitor statistics produced
show that the attractions i
receive the greatest number o
complexes. These figures do n
account of the numbers who
attractions where no turnstiles ar
count them. However the popula
following complexes is clear from t
figures.

Leisure Complex	Number of visitors in 1990
Oakwood Park, Dyfed	370 000
Barry Island Log Flume	400 000
Newport Leisure Complex	700 000
Swansea Leisure Complex	800 000

Oakwood Adventure and Leisure Park, at Haverfordwest in Dyfed, has an all-inclusive admission price for the fairground rides, bobsleigh run, puppet music hall show, go-karts, skyleap and numerous other attractions set in 80 acres of parkland. Barry Island Pleasure Park, in South Glamorgan, has over 50 rides as well as its famous log flume. The park is on the seafront and overlooks the sands of Whitmore Bay. A special attraction for families are two evenings a week set aside for their exclusive enjoyment during the summer months. The Leisure Complexes in Newport and Swansea are centres for swimming, sport, entertainment and recreation. Developed with local residents in mind, both complexes nevertheless draw visitors to their all-weather facilities.

public. The Llywernog Silver-Lead Mine at Ponterwyd in Dyfed has a miners' trail, underground tunnels, working water wheels and displays. The Dolaucathi Gold Mines at Pumsaint, also in Dyfed, allow visitors to tour the underground workings which were once mined by the Romans. The Big Pit Mining Museum at Blaenavon in Gwent closed as a working mine in 1980 but 10 years later welcomed over 100 000 visitors to descend the 300-foot shaft, complete with helmet and cap lamp.

The Welsh Miners Museum in the Afan Argoed Country Park in West Glamorgan gives a vivid picture of mining life with coal faces, pit gear and miners' equipment. The Kidwelly Industrial Museum in Dyfed has exhibitions in the original buildings relating to both tinplate and coal mining. Opened in 1989, the exhibits at the Ynysfach Engine House focus on the iron industry in the area around Merthyr Tydfil in Mid Glamorgan.

Maritime history too is represented in the ports of South Wales. The Welsh Industrial and Maritime Museum in Cardiff is situated in the docklands where displays, mock street scenes and a typical Cardiff tramp steamer combine to portray the history of the area. The Swansea Maritime and Industrial Museum is also situated in docklands and it has a selection of floating boats which attracted over 200 000 visitors in 1990.

Modern technology also draws visitors in South Wales. The Centre for Alternative Technology in Powys has windmills, solar panels and organic gardens. Techniquest in Cardiff claims to be the largest hands-on science centre in Wales with exhibits from fairground mirrors to high-tech computers included.

Diagram 14.1   Summary map of South Wales

◇ **Summary of attractions** ◇

Seaside resorts

Porthcawl, West Glamorgan
Saundersfoot, Dyfed
Tenby, Dyfed
New Quay, Dyfed
Aberystwyth, Dyfed

For children

Brecon Mountain Railway, Mid Glamorgan
Margam Park, Port Talbot, West Glamorgan
Oakwood Adventure and Leisure Park,
    Narbeth, Dyfed
Newport Leisure Centre, Gwent
Barry Island Pleasure Park, South Glamorgan
Swansea Leisure Centre, West Glamorgan
Penscynor Wildlife Park, Tenby, Dyfed
Manor House Wildlife Park, Tenby, Dyfed

Conservation areas

Brecon Beacons National Park
Cosmeston Lakes Country Park, South
    Glamorgan
Pembrokeshire Coast National Park
Margam Park, Port Talbot, West Glamorgan
Dan-Yr-Ogof Showcaves, near Abercraf,
    Powys
Afan Argoed Country Park, Port Talbot, West
    Glamorgan
Wye Valley AONB, Gwent
Cwmcarn Forest Drive, Newport, Gwent
Gower Peninsula AONB, West Glamorgan
Penscynor Wildlife Park, Neath, West
    Glamorgan
Offa's Dyke Long Distance Trail
Manor House Wildlife Park, Tenby, Dyfed
Welsh Hawking Centre, Barry, South
    Glamorgan

Historical heritage

Chepstow Castle, Gwent
Caldicot Castle, near Chepstow, Gwent
Pembroke Castle, Dyfed
Cardiff Castle, South Glamorgan
Caerphilly Castle, Mid Glamorgan

Powis Castle, Welshpool, Powys
Penhow Castle, Newport, Gwent
Tredegar House, Newport, Gwent
National Museum of Wales, Cardiff, South
    Glamorgan
Newport Museum and Art Gallery, Gwent
Welsh Folk Museum, St Fagans, Cardiff, South
    Glamorgan
Castle Hill Museum, Pembroke, Dyfed
WH Smith Shop, Newton, Powys
Llancaiach Fawr Manor, Nelson, Mid
    Glamorgan

Industrial heritage

Brecon Mountain Railway, Mid Glamorgan
Rhondda Valley Heritage Park, Trehafod, Mid
    Glamorgan
Welsh Miners Museum, Afan Argoed, Mid
    Glamorgan
Llywernog Silver-Lead Mines, Ponterwyd,
    Dyfed
Dolaucathi Gold Mines, Pumsaint, Dyfed
Big Pit Mining Museum, Blaenavon, Gwent
Kidwelly Industrial Museum, Dyfed
Ynysfach Engine House, Merthyr Tydfil, Mid
    Glamorgan
Welsh Industrial and Maritime Museum,
    Cardiff, South Glamorgan
Swansea Maritime and Industrial Museum,
    West Glamorgan
Centre for Alternative Technology,
    Machynlleth, Powys
Techniquest, Cardiff, South Glamorgan

Local events and festivals

March	Raft Race, Hay-on-Wye
May	Caldicot May Day Spectacular
	Festival of Literature, Hay-on-Wye
June	Wales and Border Counties Hound Show, Builth Wells
	Man and Horse Race, Llanwrtyd Wells, Powys
	Welsh Two-Day Motor Cycle Trials, Llandrindod Wells
July	Royal Welsh Agricultural Show, Builth Wells

August	Chepstow Biennial Festival		Brecon Jazz Festival
	Monmouth Festival		Brecon County Show
	Monmouthshire Show		Trotting Races, Llandrindod Wells
	Chepstow Agricultural Show	September	Four-Day Walk, Llanwrtyd Wells
	Victorian Festival Week,	October	Red Dragon 100-mile Horse
	Llandrindod Wells		Ride, Llanwrtyd Wells

15 *Northern Ireland*

Northern Ireland is a province of the United Kingdom and the area consists of six of the nine counties of Ulster, the ancient northern province of Ireland. The six counties are:

+ **Antrim**
+ **Londonderry**
+ **Tyrone**
+ **Fermanagh**
+ **Armagh**
+ **Down.**

The area is roughly the same size as Yorkshire. Belfast is the capital and the second city is Londonderry (also known as Derry). Two-thirds of Northern Ireland's inhabitants are Protestants and one-third are Roman Catholic. For the past 20 years, tourism has been adversely affected by the political and terrorist 'troubles' in the area, with the result that many people on mainland Britain are unaware of the attractions of the province.

The principal ferry links with mainland Britain are the Stranraer and Cairnryan to Larne crossings. In the summer there is a service to the Isle of Man, and the route from Liverpool to Belfast, which closed in 1989, may be re-opened. There are air links between Belfast and Edinburgh, Glasgow, Blackpool, Liverpool, Manchester, Birmingham, Leeds/Bradford, London and the Isle of Man. There are also direct air links to several destinations in Europe including Paris, Geneva, Amsterdam and Copenhagen. Road and rail links exist between the province and the Republic of Ireland, and more than 70 miles of motorway mean that visitors are never more than half an hour from the sea.

1990 was the best year for tourism in Northern Ireland since 1970 because, for the first time, visitors stayed over seven million nights, with about a third of these being holiday visitors. The main market for Northern Ireland tourism is Great Britain, followed by the Republic of Ireland, North America, Europe and then the rest of the world. In 1990 the greatest percentage increase was in visitors from Europe, but those from North America also increased substantially. About half of the visitors came to see friends and relatives, a quarter were on business trips and the rest came for holidays and shopping.

We shall consider the attractions of Northern Ireland under the headings of:

+ natural attractions, from the unique Giant's Causeway to beautiful lakes and mountains
+ historical attractions, from pre-historic monuments to medieval churches
+ North American links, in an area which saw emigration on a grand scale from the eighteenth century onwards.

Natural attractions

The mountains, dramatic coastline, forest parks and lakes of Northern Ireland make it a beautiful setting for activity holidays. Activities which are widely available include:

- fishing
- yachting
- back-packing
- walking
- pony trekking
- hill walking
- cycling
- golf (over 70 courses).

To the north of Belfast are the Glens of Antrim, nine valleys filled with rivers, waterfalls, wild flowers and birds. The most famous of these glens is Glenariff which has a fine display of flowers in the spring, while, in the summer, it is the venue for the *Feis na nGleann*, a lively festival of Irish dancing, music and sport. Further north is the dramatic coastline of Antrim and a World Heritage Site, the Giant's Causeway. This is a mass of contracted volcanic lava which forms giant stepping stones stretching out into the sea, almost like a pathway to Scotland. It was here that treasure from the wrecked Spanish Armada ship *Girona* was recovered in 1967. The treasure is now displayed in the Ulster Museum in Belfast. Portrush, a traditional seaside resort, is along this coast and close by is the Portstewart Strand, a beautiful 3-mile stretch of beach which is in the ownership of the National Trust.

Right in the centre of Ulster are the Sperrin Mountains, with marked paths for walkers. The towns of Strabane, Dungiven, Magherafelt and Newtownstewart are all within easy reach of these hills. The Sperrin Heritage Centre at Gortin has natural history and gold mining exhibits and visitors can hire a Klondike-style pan and try their luck in the iron pyrite stream.

Further south is the 50-mile long Lough Erne, a paradise for fishermen, bird-watchers and boaters alike. There is an abundance of trout, salmon and course fish, and the birds that have been spotted include terns, sandpipers, nightjars and garden warblers. The length of the lake and existence of Enniskillen, right at the midpoint, make this a popular base for cruising. Several companies hire boats to tourists who can usually navigate the lake after the minimum of instruction. Just to the west

Giant's Causeway, Northern Ireland

of Lough Erne are the Marble Arch Caves, where a guided tour and underground boat trip allow visitors to see the stalactites and stalagmites in the caves.

The largest lake in Northern Ireland, and indeed in the British Isles, is Lough Neagh, to the west of Belfast. Legend has it that the lake was created when the giant Finn McCool threw a clod of earth into the sea – the clod of earth being the Isle of Man! Eels are a delicacy in Northern Ireland and plenty are to be found in Lough Neagh. Deep sea fishing is popular in the Strangford Lough to the east of Belfast. This stretch of water gets its name from the Viking for 'violent fjord' after the way the sea rushes into the lough at high tide through the narrow inlet at Portaferry.

South of Belfast, near the border with the Republic of Ireland are the Mountains of Mourne, which were made famous in song. They cover an area of 15 miles by 8 miles and rise to over 2000 feet above sea level. From the top of Slieve Donard, at 2796 feet, it is possible to see the Isle of Man, all of Co. Down and the full length of Strangford Lough. The Mourne Countryside Centre in Newcastle offers talks and guided walks in the summer.

Both Forest and Country Parks abound in this province which cherishes its open spaces. Florence Court Forest Park in County Fermanagh is world famous as the site of the original Irish Yew tree. Some other parks are listed below:

♦ Glenariff Forest Park, Co. Antrim
♦ Gosford Forest Park, Co. Armagh
♦ Slieve Gullin Forest Park, Co. Armagh
♦ Castlewellan Forest Park, Co. Down
♦ Crawfordsburn Country Park, Co. Down
♦ Scrabo Country Park, Co. Down.

Castle Espie Centre at Comber in Co. Down has Ireland's largest collection of ducks, geese and swans. The Keeble National Nature Reserve on Rathlin Island, off the Antrim coast, is home to the island's main breeding colonies of kittiwakes, razorbills and puffins.

The Ulster Way, one of Europe's great long distance footpaths, stretches for 491 miles, almost right around the province. The dedicated walker could possibly do the whole trek in a month but the walk has been divided into smaller, well marked sections for day-trippers and walkers alike.

Historical attractions

Archaeological sites connected with the Celtic and early Christian history of Ireland are to be found throughout the province. The Standing Stones in the Sperrin Hills and the Mountsandel Fort, just a mile from Coleraine, give some slight insight into the way of life thousands of years ago. The Fort was first Celtic and then Norman, but recent excavations have unearthed flint implements dating from 7000 years ago. Downpatrick, the county town of Down, was the site of St Patrick's first stone church in Ireland, and numerous other places claim associations with the saint. Churches and cathedrals of interest are to be found in many towns but among the most unusual are the 'back-to-back' Killevy churches in Co. Armagh. These were an important nunnery founded in the fifth century, but other parts of the buildings date from the eleventh and fifteenth centuries. The monastic settlement on Devenish Island in Lough Erne is also interesting for its twelfth-century, 80-foot high round tower.

Castles abound in the area, particularly in Co. Down, ranging from Anglo-Norman motte-and-bailey earthworks to the seventeenth century Hillsborough Fort which was later extensively remodelled for feasts and entertainment. Carrickfergus Castle, in Co. Antrim, was started in 1180 and garrisoned until 1928, and is the largest and best preserved castle in Northern Ireland. Its Great Hall, impressive dungeons and 37-foot well are all of interest to visitors.

The National Trust is responsible for six large properties in Northern Ireland. Springhill, near Moneymore, in Co. Londonderry, is a seventeenth-century whitewashed manor house with family furniture, paintings and ornaments, and an extensive costume collection. Castle Coole, near Enniskillen, the family home of the Earls of Belmore, is a neoclassical house designed by James Wyatt with most furnishings dating from before 1830. Mount Stewart, in Co. Down, and Florence Court, in Co. Fermanagh, are both eighteenth-century houses with interesting fine furniture and paintings, and extensive grounds. Finally Castle Ward, near Downpatrick, and The Argory, near Moy, in Co. Armagh, are both regarded by the National Trust as fine examples of 'upstairs–

Historical attractions

Wales is internationally famous for its castles and these are well represented in South Wales from the ancient border castle at Chepstow to the Victorian embellishments of Cardiff Castle.

- Chepstow Castle is in a superb setting above the River Wye guarding the border between England and Wales. It was probably the first stone castle in Britain but was improved and added to right up to the Civil War making it interesting from an architectural point of view.
- Pembroke Castle in Dyfed was first built by the Normans but was completely rebuilt in the Middle Ages. It is famous as the birthplace of the first Tudor King and also as the site of a 7-week seige led by Cromwell during the Civil War.
- Caerphilly Castle in Mid Glamorgan and Manorbier Castle in Dyfed both date from the thirteenth century, as can be seen from their massive battlements and towers. Caerphilly is famous for the fact that one of its towers leans at an angle that would rival the Leaning Tower of Pisa, and Manorbier is beautifully located in the Pembrokeshire Coast National Park.
- Caldicot Castle in Gwent retains much of its fourteenth-century grandeur, in spite of being extensively modernised in the last century. It is popular nowadays for its museum, country park and regular medieval banquets.
- Cardiff Castle in South Glamorgan has Roman, Norman and Victorian connections. The Norman motte and keep are one of the best preserved in Europe but they contrast sharply with Victorian renovations, such as the fantasy octagonal tower.

Many of the Welsh castles are in the care of CADW, the Heritage Monuments section of the Welsh Office. This is comparable to English Heritage in England and similar entrance concessions apply to those who join CADW as to those who join English Heritage. An additional bonus for members of either organisation is that they receive free entry to properties in both England and Wales in their second and subsequent years of membership.

Penhow Castle in Gwent is Wales' oldest inhabited castle and was originally a small border fortress. Nowadays it presents a picture of life over seven centuries from the twelfth-century Great Hall to a Victorian housekeeper's room. Welsh country farmhouse feasts are provided in the tithe barn and the Visitor Centre has its own inn, the Castle Arms. Tredegar House, also in Gwent is South Wales' finest country house. Set in 90 acres of parkland, the seventeenth-century house has over 40 beautifully refurbished rooms. Carriage rides, self-guided trails, craft workshops, boating and an adventure playground all contribute to a full day's entertainment.

Powis Castle in Welshpool receives over 100 000 visitors each year. The castle was built in the thirteenth century but its country house collection includes Georgian furniture, tapestries and pictures. Many of the treasures were inherited from Clive of India, whose son married a Powis heiress.

The National Museum of Wales' main building is located in Cardiff where the collection includes paintings, silver, ceramics and archaeological artefacts. A wealth of local culture is displayed in the Welsh Folk Museum at St Fagans outside Cardiff. The old farmhouses, cottages, tannery, school and chapel of the outdoor museum were visited in 1990 by 264 897 people. The Newport Museum and Art Gallery received over 130 000 visitors in 1990, possibly drawn by the specialist displays which relate to local connections with the Chartist Movement of 1838–40.

More recent, innovative museums in South Wales include the Castle Hill Museum of the Home in Pembroke which received the Prince of Wales Award in the first year it was opened. Over 3000 artefacts related to everyday life in Wales are displayed in a domestic setting. The WH Smith 1920s shop replica in Newtown in Powys has been completely restored in its original state and is an unusual combination of museum and shop. A more recent attraction is the Llancaiach Fawr Manor in Nelson, Mid Glamorgan, where life during the era of the Civil War is brought vividly to life through events and banquets.

Industrial heritage

The mining heritage of Wales is remembered in silver, gold and coal mines which are open to the

Cardiff, we shall consider Porthcawl, Saundersfoot and Tenby, and moving up the west coast, north of Cardigan, we shall look at New Quay and Aberystwyth.

♦ Porthcawl has two south facing beaches at Sandy Bay and Trecco Bay. The Coney Beach amusement complex, waterslides and splash pool are open all day and a range of entertainment is provided in the evening at the Grand Pavilion on the Esplanade. Either side of the resort is the solitude of sand dunes and only 5 miles away at Ogmore is the start of the Glamorgan Heritage Coast where the cliffs have been eroded by the sea into strange, spectacular shapes.

♦ Saundersfoot developed as a resort from an eighteenth-century fishing village and coal port. The resort's history gives it some original features such as a Barbecue Restaurant which was originally the colliery offices. The 3 miles of sandy beach are backed by shops, a peaceful park and cliff walks. Fresh fish is landed at the harbour each day, and boats can be chartered by more adventurous visitors.

♦ Tenby is Saundersfoot's brasher neighbour, which offers everything one would expect in a modern holiday resort. The town has four beaches and a picturesque harbour. The winding alleys of the small medieval town add to the enjoyment of a family holiday.

♦ New Quay is a picturesque fishing village with terraced cottages clinging to its steep cliffs which descend sharply to the beach and harbour. Dylan Thomas lived near New Quay and he is said to have referred to the resort in *Under Milk Wood* as the 'cliff-perched town at the far end of Wales'. The high cliffs afford visitors spectacular views of Cardigan Bay.

♦ Aberystwyth is the largest town and principal shopping centre of Mid Wales, as well as being an ideal centre for touring the region. At the northern end of the promenade is the longest electric cliff railway in Britain, and, in the summer, the Vale of Rheidol narrow gauge steam railway takes visitors 680 feet up the hillside along the 12-mile track. As well as being a popular holiday destination, Aberystwyth has the National Library of Wales and the Ceredigion Museum, which is housed in a restored music hall.

We have seen that natural attractions in South Wales include the mountains as well as the coastline and, as a result, inland as well as seaside resorts have developed in the area. One such inland resort is Llandrindod Wells, a spa town in Powys, which first became popular in the nineteenth century when the railway arrived. The town's Victorian Festival in August reflects its past and has an ideal setting in the Victorian architecture of the town. During the week of the Festival, shop assistants, railway staff, postal staff and hotel staff all don Victorian costume, and cars are banned from the main streets, being replaced by horses and carriages. Situated 700 feet above sea level, Llandrindod Wells is surrounded by some of the most beautiful countryside in Wales and is an ideal touring base.

Visitor statistics produced by the Tourist Councils show that the attractions in South Wales which receive the greatest number of visitors are leisure complexes. These figures do not of course take account of the numbers who visit natural attractions where no turnstiles are available to count them. However the popularity of the following complexes is clear from the visitor figures.

Leisure Complex	Number of visitors in 1990
Oakwood Park, Dyfed	370 000
Barry Island Log Flume	400 000
Newport Leisure Complex	700 000
Swansea Leisure Complex	800 000

Oakwood Adventure and Leisure Park, at Haverfordwest in Dyfed, has an all-inclusive admission price for the fairground rides, bobsleigh run, puppet music hall show, go-karts, skyleap and numerous other attractions set in 80 acres of parkland. Barry Island Pleasure Park, in South Glamorgan, has over 50 rides as well as its famous log flume. The park is on the seafront and overlooks the sands of Whitmore Bay. A special attraction for families are two evenings a week set aside for their exclusive enjoyment during the summer months. The Leisure Complexes in Newport and Swansea are centres for swimming, sport, entertainment and recreation. Developed with local residents in mind, both complexes nevertheless draw visitors to their all-weather facilities.

Swansea, is a haven of tranquillity where the sea is never far away and rocky headlands, such as the Mumbles, often hide tiny sandy beaches which were once the haunt of smugglers.

Offa's Dyke is one of the most famous Long Distance Trails in the UK. It follows the route of the boundary dyke built by Offa, King of Mercia in the eighth century. Starting at the Sedbury Cliffs south of Chepstow in Gwent, it covers 168 miles to the River Dee in Clwyd. There is an Offa's Dyke Information and Heritage Centre at Knighton in Powys which has a range of publications, library, slide shows and exhibitions related to walking in the area.

In an area renowned for its beauty it is not surprising to find several Country Parks. These include:

- Cosmeston Lakes Country Park in South Glamorgan, which covers over 200 acres of lakes, woodland and meadows. The park was formerly a limestone quarry but was landscaped and developed as a leisure centre during the 1980s. A unique feature of the park is its medieval village which has been excavated and reconstructed on its original site.
- Margam Park near Port Talbot in West Glamorgan received over 250 000 visitors in 1990. The park covers 800 acres within which are the impressive castle, an adventure playground, a miniature nursery rhyme village, one of Europe's largest mazes, orangery gardens, putting and giant chess. A programme of events throughout the year ensures a variety of entertainment, from craft fairs to military displays.
- Afan Argoed Country Park, also near Port Talbot, is set in a beautiful deep sided forested valley which is known locally as 'little Switzerland'. Countryside and forestry walks are well signposted and a cycle hire centre helps visitors make full use of a 14-mile cycle way. Within the park is the Welsh Miners Museum which we shall consider later in this chapter.

Cwmcarn Forest Drive is a 7-mile scenic route, which was developed by the Forestry Commission for motorists through Gwent. The route offers spectacular views over the Bristol Channel, and a number of picnic sites with play areas, barbecues and forest walks have been provided.

Wildlife Parks are popular in South Wales. The most frequently visited in 1990 was Penscynor Wildlife Park at Cilfrew in West Glamorgan, which received over 280 000 visitors. Animals in the park include chimpanzees, monkeys, penguins and tropical birds. Play areas, a chairlift and an alpine slide all contribute to enjoyment for a family day out. Manor House Wildlife and Leisure Park at St Florence, near Tenby, in Dyfed received over 100 000 visitors in 1990. Falconry is a special attraction at this park, as well as an animal and bird collection, attractive gardens and a model railway. The Welsh Hawking Centre at Barry in South Glamorgan has over 200 birds of prey, including eagles, owls, buzzards, hawks and falcons.

◇ **Activity:** *Countryside walking tour* ◇

In such a beautiful area as South Wales there could be another Long Distance Trail. Consider the natural attractions of the area and consult the terrain, using an Ordnance Survey Map.

Choose a specific area of at least 400 square miles or 1000 square kilometres and design a countryside route which could be walked in about a week. Break the walk into sections which can be covered in a day, and consider places for overnight stops.

Summarise your walking tour on an illustrated map which indicates:

- distance
- terrain
- particular natural attractions
- other attractions
- main accommodation points for overnight stops.

Resorts and family entertainment

Many seaside resorts in South Wales are as yet unspoilt by commercialisation and certainly none could be regarded as meccas of loud entertainment. Along the south coast, west of

Natural attractions

Two of the 11 National Parks of England and Wales are in this area, namely the Brecon Beacons National Park and the Pembrokeshire Coast National Park. The Brecon Beacons has open moorland, gentle pastures and lonely mountain summits, and the Park's limestone cliffs have interesting caves, hidden streams and some of the most spectacular waterfalls in the British Isles. The Dan-Yr-Ogof Showcaves at Abercraf, midway between Brecon and Swansea, have received nine tourism awards in recent years. In 1990 the caves welcomed 200 000 visitors to see the Cathedral Showcave, the largest single chamber of any British showcave, and the Bone Cave which was inhabited by humans 3000 years ago. The Brecon Mountain Railway's 1-hour trip covers 4 miles of beautiful scenery along the side of the Taf Fechan Reservoir, and the Brecon Beacons Mountain Centre at Libanus receives over 100 000 visitors each year.

The Pembrokeshire Coast National Park covers 180 miles of coastline, from St Dogmaels near Cardigan to Amroth near Tenby. The Park has islands, sand dunes and impressive cliffs, with associated bird life. Two of the islands hold the largest breeding colonies of puffins in southern Britain. Skokholm holds about 2500 pairs of puffins, and Skomer has an even larger colony with 6000. In both National Parks there is a Ranger Service which provides facilities such as guided walks for all abilities, and discovery days, for a variety of interests.

There are also two designated Areas of Outstanding Natural Beauty (AONB) in South Wales, namely the Wye Valley and the Gower Peninsula. Chepstow and Monmouth are both ideal centres for holidays in the Wye Valley. Tintern Abbey, which is located halfway between the two towns, epitomises the beauty of this area with its splendid peaceful scenery of green wooded slopes in the summer and golden tints in the autumn. The Gower Peninsula, to the west of

Pembrokeshire Coast National Park

public. The Llywernog Silver-Lead Mine at Ponterwyd in Dyfed has a miners' trail, underground tunnels, working water wheels and displays. The Dolaucathi Gold Mines at Pumsaint, also in Dyfed, allow visitors to tour the underground workings which were once mined by the Romans. The Big Pit Mining Museum at Blaenavon in Gwent closed as a working mine in 1980 but 10 years later welcomed over 100 000 visitors to descend the 300-foot shaft, complete with helmet and cap lamp.

The Welsh Miners Museum in the Afan Argoed Country Park in West Glamorgan gives a vivid picture of mining life with coal faces, pit gear and miners' equipment. The Kidwelly Industrial Museum in Dyfed has exhibitions in the original buildings relating to both tinplate and coal mining. Opened in 1989, the exhibits at the Ynysfach Engine House focus on the iron industry in the area around Merthyr Tydfil in Mid Glamorgan.

Maritime history too is represented in the ports of South Wales. The Welsh Industrial and Maritime Museum in Cardiff is situated in the docklands where displays, mock street scenes and a typical Cardiff tramp steamer combine to portray the history of the area. The Swansea Maritime and Industrial Museum is also situated in docklands and it has a selection of floating boats which attracted over 200 000 visitors in 1990.

Modern technology also draws visitors in South Wales. The Centre for Alternative Technology in Powys has windmills, solar panels and organic gardens. Techniquest in Cardiff claims to be the largest hands-on science centre in Wales with exhibits from fairground mirrors to high-tech computers included.

Diagram 14.1   Summary map of South Wales

◇ **Summary of attractions** ◇

Seaside resorts

Porthcawl, West Glamorgan
Saundersfoot, Dyfed
Tenby, Dyfed
New Quay, Dyfed
Aberystwyth, Dyfed

For children

Brecon Mountain Railway, Mid Glamorgan
Margam Park, Port Talbot, West Glamorgan
Oakwood Adventure and Leisure Park,
    Narbeth, Dyfed
Newport Leisure Centre, Gwent
Barry Island Pleasure Park, South Glamorgan
Swansea Leisure Centre, West Glamorgan
Penscynor Wildlife Park, Tenby, Dyfed
Manor House Wildlife Park, Tenby, Dyfed

Conservation areas

Brecon Beacons National Park
Cosmeston Lakes Country Park, South
    Glamorgan
Pembrokeshire Coast National Park
Margam Park, Port Talbot, West Glamorgan
Dan-Yr-Ogof Showcaves, near Abercraf,
    Powys
Afan Argoed Country Park, Port Talbot, West
    Glamorgan
Wye Valley AONB, Gwent
Cwmcarn Forest Drive, Newport, Gwent
Gower Peninsula AONB, West Glamorgan
Penscynor Wildlife Park, Neath, West
    Glamorgan
Offa's Dyke Long Distance Trail
Manor House Wildlife Park, Tenby, Dyfed
Welsh Hawking Centre, Barry, South
    Glamorgan

Historical heritage

Chepstow Castle, Gwent
Caldicot Castle, near Chepstow, Gwent
Pembroke Castle, Dyfed
Cardiff Castle, South Glamorgan
Caerphilly Castle, Mid Glamorgan

Powis Castle, Welshpool, Powys
Penhow Castle, Newport, Gwent
Tredegar House, Newport, Gwent
National Museum of Wales, Cardiff, South
    Glamorgan
Newport Museum and Art Gallery, Gwent
Welsh Folk Museum, St Fagans, Cardiff, South
    Glamorgan
Castle Hill Museum, Pembroke, Dyfed
WH Smith Shop, Newton, Powys
Llancaiach Fawr Manor, Nelson, Mid
    Glamorgan

Industrial heritage

Brecon Mountain Railway, Mid Glamorgan
Rhondda Valley Heritage Park, Trehafod, Mid
    Glamorgan
Welsh Miners Museum, Afan Argoed, Mid
    Glamorgan
Llywernog Silver-Lead Mines, Ponterwyd,
    Dyfed
Dolaucathi Gold Mines, Pumsaint, Dyfed
Big Pit Mining Museum, Blaenavon, Gwent
Kidwelly Industrial Museum, Dyfed
Ynysfach Engine House, Merthyr Tydfil, Mid
    Glamorgan
Welsh Industrial and Maritime Museum,
    Cardiff, South Glamorgan
Swansea Maritime and Industrial Museum,
    West Glamorgan
Centre for Alternative Technology,
    Machynlleth, Powys
Techniquest, Cardiff, South Glamorgan

Local events and festivals

March	Raft Race, Hay-on-Wye
May	Caldicot May Day Spectacular
	Festival of Literature, Hay-on-Wye
June	Wales and Border Counties Hound Show, Builth Wells
	Man and Horse Race, Llanwrtyd Wells, Powys
	Welsh Two-Day Motor Cycle Trials, Llandrindod Wells
July	Royal Welsh Agricultural Show, Builth Wells

August	Chepstow Biennial Festival		Brecon Jazz Festival
	Monmouth Festival		Brecon County Show
	Monmouthshire Show		Trotting Races, Llandrindod Wells
	Chepstow Agricultural Show	September	Four-Day Walk, Llanwrtyd Wells
	Victorian Festival Week,	October	Red Dragon 100-mile Horse
	Llandrindod Wells		Ride, Llanwrtyd Wells

15 *Northern Ireland*

Northern Ireland is a province of the United Kingdom and the area consists of six of the nine counties of Ulster, the ancient northern province of Ireland. The six counties are:

- **Antrim**
- **Londonderry**
- **Tyrone**
- **Fermanagh**
- **Armagh**
- **Down.**

The area is roughly the same size as Yorkshire. Belfast is the capital and the second city is Londonderry (also known as Derry). Two-thirds of Northern Ireland's inhabitants are Protestants and one-third are Roman Catholic. For the past 20 years, tourism has been adversely affected by the political and terrorist 'troubles' in the area, with the result that many people on mainland Britain are unaware of the attractions of the province.

The principal ferry links with mainland Britain are the Stranraer and Cairnryan to Larne crossings. In the summer there is a service to the Isle of Man, and the route from Liverpool to Belfast, which closed in 1989, may be re-opened. There are air links between Belfast and Edinburgh, Glasgow, Blackpool, Liverpool, Manchester, Birmingham, Leeds/Bradford, London and the Isle of Man. There are also direct air links to several destinations in Europe including Paris, Geneva, Amsterdam and Copenhagen. Road and rail links exist between the province and the Republic of Ireland, and more than 70 miles of motorway mean that visitors are never more than half an hour from the sea.

1990 was the best year for tourism in Northern Ireland since 1970 because, for the first time, visitors stayed over seven million nights, with about a third of these being holiday visitors. The main market for Northern Ireland tourism is Great Britain, followed by the Republic of Ireland, North America, Europe and then the rest of the world. In 1990 the greatest percentage increase was in visitors from Europe, but those from North America also increased substantially. About half of the visitors came to see friends and relatives, a quarter were on business trips and the rest came for holidays and shopping.

We shall consider the attractions of Northern Ireland under the headings of:

- natural attractions, from the unique Giant's Causeway to beautiful lakes and mountains
- historical attractions, from pre-historic monuments to medieval churches
- North American links, in an area which saw emigration on a grand scale from the eighteenth century onwards.

Natural attractions

The mountains, dramatic coastline, forest parks and lakes of Northern Ireland make it a beautiful downstairs' houses which vividly portray life in a Victorian country house.

The Ulster Folk and Transport Museum at Cultra, in Co. Down, can be easily reached by public transport from Belfast. Here, a nineteenth-century village has been re-created with houses, cottages, and a tiny church, moved from other parts of the province. Horse drawn ploughs are used to help create an authentic rural atmosphere, and demonstrations of weaving, spinning and thatching take place throughout the summer. The transport section of the museum has every kind of vehicle on display, from donkeys to aircraft.

◇ **Activity:** *Presentation* ◇

Write to the Northern Ireland Tourist Board at
River House
48 High Street
Belfast BT1 2DS

and request information about the attractions of Northern Ireland.

While you are waiting for the material to arrive, carry out a short survey in your area to establish the knowledge and opinions of local people with regard to Northern Ireland.

Bearing in mind the answers to your survey, mount an exhibition or presentation on the attractions of Northern Ireland. You may even be able to do this activity in cooperation with a local travel agent.

North American links

In the eighteenth century thousands of emigrants left from Belfast and Larne on their way to new lives in Canada, America, New Zealand and Australia. Mark Twain's ancestors came from Ballyclare and Davy Crockett, Edgar Allan Poe and Paul Getty all had Ulster ancestors. Many visitors from USA and Canada wish to trace their Ulster roots and several companies have been set up to deliver heritage holidays offering advice on ancestry.

The Northern Ireland Tourist Board says that it is a well known fact that the forbears of a dozen American presidents emigrated from Ulster, mostly in the eighteenth century. In fact men of Ulster descent occupied the White House for 56 of the 92 years between the inauguration of Andrew Jackson and the termination of Woodrow Wilson's eight years in office. The Andrew Jackson Centre, at Boneybefore near Belfast is a replica of the cottage in which Jackson's parents lived. The ancestors of Ulysses Grant, a hero of the Civil War and later president, came from Aughnacloy in Co. Tyrone where a plaque on the wall marks the house. From Strabane, Co. Tyrone the grandfather of Woodrow Wilson, 28th president of the United States, emigrated at the beginning of the last century. Wilsons still live in the ancestral home, a modest farmhouse, and members of the family will show callers around the house.

Pogue's Entry in Antrim was the childhood home of Alexander Irvine who became a missionary in New York's Bowery. He immortalised the ups and downs of Irish country life in his book *My Lady of the Chimney Corner*. The Earhart Centre in Londonderry is a cottage exhibition commemorating Amelia Earhart, the first woman to fly the Atlantic solo, landing near the site in 1932.

The Ulster American Folk Park at Camphill near Omagh in Co. Tyrone brings to life the conditions on ships and dockside at the time of the mass emigrations. With his family, Thomas Mellon emigrated, at the age of five, from Camphill in 1818 and later became a judge, banker and father of Andrew Mellon the multimillionaire developer of Pittsburgh. The Mellon family provided funds for the development of the site which has 'old' and 'new' world sections contrasting life in Ireland and in America, complete with schoolhouse, forge and stockade.

Many American tourists visit the Giant's Causeway, described earlier, and the nearest town of Bushmills holds its own unique attraction in the oldest licensed whiskey distillery in the world. Irish whiskey is spelt with an 'e' before the 'y', unlike Scotch whisky, from which it also differs in colour and taste. Visitors are welcomed on a tour of the factory, with a tasting session included.

Diagram 15.1   Summary map of Northern Ireland

◇ **Summary of attractions** ◇

Seaside resorts

Portrush, Co. Antrim
Bangor, Co. Down

Family attactions

Sperrin Heritage Centre, Gortin, Co. Tyrone
Ulster Folk and Transport Museum, Cultra,
    near Belfast, Co. Down
Ulster American Folk Park, Omagh, Co. Tyrone

Conservation areas

Glens of Antrim
Lough Erne, Co. Fermanagh

Giant's Causeway, Co. Antrim
Lough Neagh, Co. Down
Portstewart Strand, Co. Londonderry
Marble Arch Caves, Florence Court, Co.
    Fermanagh
Florence Court Forest Park, Co. Fermanagh
Castle Espie Bird Centre, Comber, Co. Down
Glenariff Forest Park, Co. Antrim
Rathlin Island Bird Sanctuary
Gosford Forest Park, Co. Armagh
Slieve Gullin Forest Park, Co. Armagh
Castlewellan Forest Park, Co. Fermanagh
Crawfordsburn Country Park, Co. Down
Scrabo Country Park, Co. Down
The Ulster Way Footpath

Historical attractions

Ulster Museum, Belfast
Mountsandel Fort, Coleraine, Co. Antrim
Carrickfergus Castle, Co. Antrim
Springhill, Moneymore, Co. Londonderry
Castle Coole, Enniskillen, Co. Fermanagh
Mount Stewart, Co. Down
Florence Court, Co. Fermanagh
Castle Ward, Downpatrick, Co. Down
The Argory, Moy, Co. Armanagh
Ulster Folk and Transport Museum, Cultra, Co. Down
Ulster American Folk Park, Omagh, Co. Tyrone

Local events and feastivals

March 17	St Patrick's Day
May	The Lord Mayor's Show, Belfast
	North-West 200, motorcycle race
	Fishing Festival, Fermanagh Lakeland
	Royal Ulster Agricultural Show, Belfast
June	*Feis na nGleann*, Glens of Antrim
July	World Rose Convention, Belfast
July 12	Orangemen's Day
August	Relief of Derry Celebrations
	Oul' Lammas Fair, Ballycastle
September	World Ploughing Championships, Limavady

16 *The Channel Islands*

The Channel Islands are not strictly speaking part of the UK but they have been included in this volume because British tourists regard them as part of the British Isles. In fact the Bailiwicks, or Districts, of Guernsey and Jersey are independent jurisdictions, once the domain of the Duchy of Normandy, and now loyal directly to the English Crown. The islands have their own laws and taxes and have no representatives in the British Parliament and so, with regard to government, the Channel Islands are quite different from Wales, Scotland or Northern Ireland. Physically, the islands form part of north west France, and French is widely spoken, but when islanders talk about the 'mainland' they mean the UK, to which they are bound by centuries-old ties. Under a special protocol to Britain's Treaty of Accession to the European Community, Guernsey and Jersey are within the EC for the purposes of trade, but out of it for almost everything else, including financial aid.

There are several islands in the group, some private, others uninhabited, but from the point of view of British tourists there are five popular islands. These are Jersey, the busiest of the islands, and Guernsey with Alderney, Herm and Sark, the islands within its Bailiwick. While the smaller islands acknowledge the Bailiff of Guernsey as their civil head and chief of justice, they also retain their own independence in varying degrees.

The economy of the islands is self supporting and tourism plays an increasingly important role. Surveys are carried out approximately every five years on Jersey and Guernsey and these show that Jersey attracts about 1.25 million visitors a year, of whom 80 per cent are British, and Guernsey attracts about 250 000 visitors, of whom 91 per cent are UK holidaymakers. British visitors come mainly from London and the south east and are on average over 45 years of age. Increasingly, holidays are being taken out of season, with autumn the more popular time. Jersey is the island nearest to France and French visitors account for about 13 per cent of its visitors. These French holidaymakers tend to come from Paris, Normandy or Brittany. The attraction of the islands is that to the French they represent a little bit of England and to the British they seem very French. It was the French writer Victor Hugo who described the Channel Islands as 'pieces of France fallen into the sea and picked up by England'.

Most British visitors tend to arrive in the Channel Islands by air on package holidays. There are international airports on Guernsey, 3 miles from the capital St Peter Port, and on Jersey at St Peter's airport, 5 miles from the capital St Helier. Most French tourists arrive by sea for independent holidays. Ferries connect the islands to the French ports of St Malo, Cherbourg and Carteret as well as to the English ports of Portsmouth, Weymouth and, in the summer, Torquay. An inter-island service connects the islands of Herm, Sark and Alderney with their larger neighbours.

Jersey

Covering approximately 45 square miles, Jersey is the busiest of the Channel Islands. For many visitors the island's main attraction is its natural beauty of country lanes, cultivated fields, cliff top walks and uncrowded beaches. Walking is a pleasure in such scenery and there are several designated paths, including the Old Jersey Railway which is now a 4-mile public footpath from St Aubin to Corbière. There are beaches all around the island and these vary from the sheltered bay, rocks and pools of Plêmont to the 5-mile beach at St Ouen's Bay, which is popular with surfers. It is possible to find most water sports around the coast, including windsurfing, waterskiing, sub aqua diving and traditional swimming or fishing. Bird-watching too is popular, with sites of interest on the north and east coasts in the summer, and on the south coast in the winter. St Ouen's Bay on the west of the island has been designated a nature reserve.

St Helier, the capital, and by far the biggest town on Jersey, is overlooked by the sixteenth-century Elizabeth Castle, which can be approached on foot at low tide or by a DUKW ferry service. The castle was named after Queen Elizabeth I by Sir Walter Raleigh, while he was Governor of Jersey. Elizabeth Castle has a chequered history, having survived a seige by Cromwell in 1651, and occupation by German forces during World War II. Fort Regent, which was built on an outcrop above the town, has been converted into a modern leisure complex with a swimming pool, indoor sports, a funfair and piazza stage shows. St Helier is particularly popular with British tourists for shopping. No VAT and low duty on goods make perfume, cosmetics, watches and jewellery bargain buys for visitors.

Apart from the natural beauty of the island, the following are the main attractions outside St Helier.

♦ The Jersey Zoological Park at Les Augres Manor, is the home of Gerald Durrell and the Jersey Wildlife Preservation Trust, a worldwide organisation dedicated to the conservation of endangered species. Some of the rarest birds and reptiles are to be seen in the 25 acres of beautiful parkland.
♦ Samarès Manor in St Clement, is a beautiful house, standing in 14 acres of grounds. Of special interest are the herb garden, with over a hundred species, and the Japanese garden, with a series of cascading waterfalls.
♦ Mont Orgueil Castle, at Gorey, dominates the east coast on a site which has been fortified since the Iron Age. The castle is one of the best preserved examples of a medieval concentric design and a series of tableaux take visitors through the history of the building.

Fort Regent

♦ The German Underground Hospital was tunnelled out of solid rock by prisoners of war and civilians during the German Occupation, 1940–45. Lighting and special effects re-create working conditions, and photographs, a collection of German firearms and an escapee's boat are on display.

Guernsey

Covering 80 square miles, Guernsey is the largest of the Channel Islands. Referred to as the 'green island', its attraction lies in peace and relaxation rather than entertainment. The uniqueness of the island is demonstrated with its blue post boxes, yellow telephone boxes and French signposts. Trips to Herm and Sark or to mainland France often form part of a holiday for British visitors.

Bird-watching, rambling, fishing and walking are all ideal pursuits along the rocky coastline of Guernsey. The South Cliff Path covers 16 miles through pine woods with spectacular views of the sea and can be walked energetically in a day. However, the walk has been broken into manageable sections with headland car parks at intervals. Inland, there is a network of over 300 miles of roads and lanes. Water lanes, which have a stream running down the middle or to one side, are a special feature of Guernsey. There are a number of nature reserves around the island including the Quanteraine Valley, inland from Rocquaine Bay on the west coast.

Guernsey beaches are usually comparatively deserted as there are limited parking facilities at most sites and strict regulations against driving on the beaches in the summer. Rocquaine Bay is the venue for the Summer Regatta; Fermain Bay, 2 miles south of St Peter Port, can only be reached by a 30-minute boat trip or a walk along the cliffs; and Moulin Huet on the south coast was chosen as a painting site by Renoir and now has a pottery workshop which is open to the public. Traditional harbours around the coast such as Grand Havre in the north and Bordeaux Harbour in the east make a picturesque setting for tourists and painters alike. Windsurfing is popular at the northern beaches of Pembroke Bay, Ladies Bay, L'Ancresse, Vazon and Cobo Bay. Waterskiing is a special attraction in Havelet Bay just south of St Peter Port.

St Peter Port, the capital, is an attractive town with numerous bistros, bars and cafes in its winding streets. Shopping is a particular attraction in the pedestrianised streets and Victorian market hall. Old Guernsey Markets are held every Thursday in the Market Square during the summer, when stall holders and helpers wear traditional Guernsey costume, and the day is rounded off with square dancing in the evening. The Beau Séjour leisure complex, set in parkland overlooking the town, has modern amenities from swimming to sports and a theatre. The great walls of Castle Cornet dominate the harbour entrance. The castle is floodlit at night and a gun is fired at noon each day from its thirteenth-century battlements. The Guernsey Museum and Art Gallery in St Peter Port was opened in 1978 to portray the history of Guernsey and its people. Hauteville House, the home of the famous nineteenth-century writer Victor Hugo is maintained as a museum by the City of Paris and guided tours are available for parties of 15 people at a time.

Apart from the natural beauty of the island, the following are the main attractions outside St Peter Port.

♦ Fort Grey at Rocquaine Bay was built in 1804 as part of the defences against Napoleon and is known locally as the 'cup and saucer' due to the shape of its tower. The fort is now a maritime museum with a special feature about shipwrecks on the treacherous Hanois Reef.
♦ The German Occupation Museum just south of the airport has tableaux, bunker rooms and a full-scale street telling the story of the Nazi occupation of Guernsey from 1940–45.
♦ Further north, in the centre of the island is the German Underground Hospital, an austere and chilly series of tunnels excavated by slave labour and intended as a hospital and munitions store.
♦ La Vallette is also a tunnel complex, excavated in St Peter Port as a fuel store for U-boats. The complex now houses the Guernsey Military Museum and has received the *Welcome to Britain Award* of the British Tourist Authority.
♦ Sausmarez Manor, inland from Fermain Bay on the east coast, is a time capsule of unusual items. The collection includes King James II's wedding suit and the manor is set in exotic gardens.

◆ On a site further north, towards Cobo Bay, the Saumarez Park Folk Museum has been developed by the National Trust of Guernsey around an eighteenth-century farm courtyard. The museum has a series of period rooms including a dairy, cider barn, wash house and tool room. On the evening of the first Monday in July *Le Viaër Marchi*, or The Old Market, takes place in the grounds of the museum with stalls, crafts, dancing and traditional food.

◇ **Activity:** *Giving comparative advice* ◇

To prepare for a special promotion on the Channel Islands you have been given the task of drawing up a comparative table of the attractions of Jersey and Guernsey.

Use the information given above and resources from libraries and the Tourist Boards to compile a table comparing and contrasting the attractions of the islands.

You may wish to consider the following topics.

	Jersey	Guernsey
airports		
ferry links		
climate		
shopping facilities		
sports facilities		
accommodation		
accommodation price range		
nature reserves		
designated footpaths		
historical attractions		
special events		

The table should be produced in such a way that it would be a useful quick reference should you be giving advice to a person who was undecided about which island would suit their holiday requirements.

Once completed, you could test the usefulness of your table in a role play with colleagues.

Smaller islands

Herm is just 3 miles east of Guernsey and can only be reached by sea. Just 1.5 miles long, the island is traffic free and has only 50 resident adults, one hotel, a restaurant, an inn, a tiny Norman chapel and a shopping piazza. In keeping with the isolation and peace of the island there is no bank, the hotel rooms do not have televisions or telephones, and transistor radios are not permitted to be played in public places.

With one of the largest dairy farms in the Channel Islands, the landscape is peaceful and attractive. Shell Beach on the east coast is unique with hundreds of varieties of shells washed up by the Gulf Stream. The habitat of the island is ideal for a tremendous variety of birds, including puffin.

Sark is 40 minutes by launch to the east of Guernsey. This tiny feudal state is a world on its own with traditions and laws reminiscent of 100 years ago. The island is traffic free, the local taxi is a horse-drawn carriage and the ambulance and fire engine are drawn by tractor.

Sark's constitution dates back to the reign of Queen Elizabeth I and the present hereditary ruler, the *Seigneur*, is Michael Beaumont. The Court of Chief Pleas legislates on local matters and there is no income tax or death duties on Sark. The island has a population of approximately 500 adults, six hotels, several guest houses and self catering and camping facilities. It is a rambler's paradise, particularly along the coastline, with spectacular 300-foot cliffs in places. La Coupée in particular is a narrow, high 'cat walk' which joins the main island to Little Sark in the south.

Alderney is about 20 miles north of Guernsey and the closest of the Channel Islands to both England and France. The island is 3.5 miles long by 1.5 miles wide and has a population of approximately 2000, 76 per cent of whom are settlers from the UK. The island has its own airport, and the only railway in the Channel Islands, which is run as a tourist attraction along a 2-mile stretch of track.

There are several bars and restaurants in the cobbled streets of the town of St Anne and most of the white sandy beaches are uncrowded even in summer. The island is considered a naturalist's paradise with large colonies of gannets and puffins.

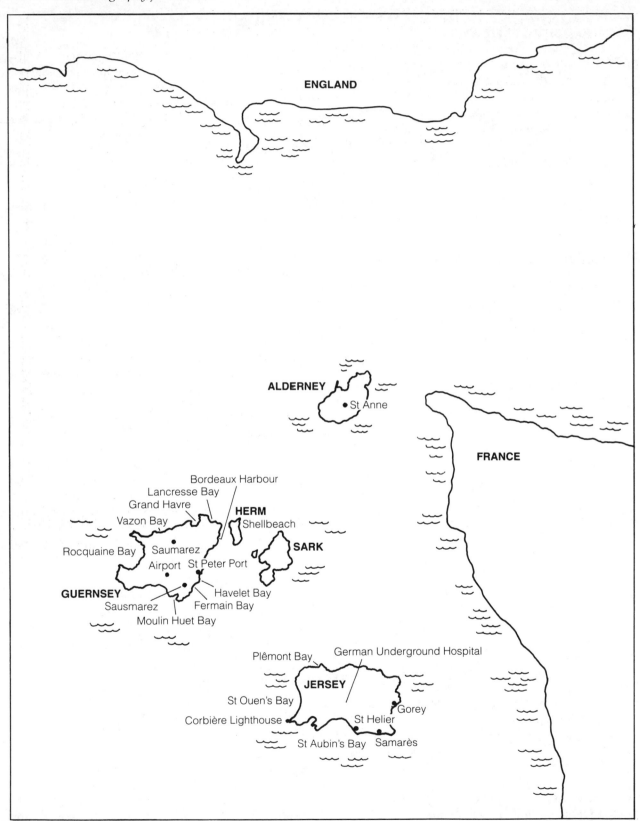

Diagram 16.1   Summary map of the Channel Islands

◇   Summary of attractions   ◇

For children

Beaches on all islands
Shell Beach, Herm
Fort Regent leisure complex, Jersey
Beau Séjour leisure complex, Guernsey

Conservation areas

Old Jersey Railway Path
St Ouen's Bay, Jersey
Jersey Zoological Park
South Cliff Path, Guernsey
Quanteraine Valley, Guernsey

Historical heritage

Elizabeth Castle, Jersey
Samarès Manor, Jersey
Mont Orgueil Castle, Jersey
Castle Cornet, Guernsey
Guernsey Museum and Art Gallery
Hauteville House, Guernsey
Fort Grey Museum, Guernsey
La Vallette, Guernsey
German Occupation Museum, Guernsey
German Underground Hospitals, Jersey and
    Guernsey
Saumarez Park Folk Museum, Guernsey
Sausmarez Manor, Guernsey

Local events and festivals

April	Festival France/Jersey
May	International Air Rally, Jersey
9 May	Liberation Day
May–September	Old Guernsey Market, every Thursday
June	International Dance Festival, Guernsey
	Jersey Fair
July	Rocquaine Regatta, Guernsey
	Le Viaër Marchi, Saumarez Folk Park, Guernsey
August	Festival of Flowers, Jersey (second Thursday)
	Festival of Flowers, Guernsey (last week)
September	International Power Boat Week, Guernsey
October	Chess Festival, Guernsey
November	Half Marathon, Jersey

Appendix

Useful addresses

Association of Scottish Visitor Attractions
Camasunary
Kidsneuk
Irvine
Ayrshire KA12 8SR

British Resorts Association
PO Box 9
Margate
Thanet
Kent CT9 1XZ

British Spas Federation
Wychavon District Council
37 High Street
Pershore
Worcs WR10 1AH

British Tourist Authority
Thames Tower
Black's Road
London W6 9EL

British Travel Educational Trust
24 Grosvenor Gardens
London SW1W 0ET

British Waterways
Greycaine Road
Watford
Herts WD2 4JR

CADW: Welsh Historic Monuments
Brunel House
2 Fitzalan Road
Cardiff CF2 1UY

Civic Trust
17 Carlton House Terrace
London SW1Y 5AW

Council for the Protection of Rural England
Warwick House
25 Buckingham Palace Road
London SW1W 0PP

Council for the Protection of Rural Wales
Tŷ Gwyn
31 High Street
Welshpool
Powys ST21 7JP

The Countryside Commission
John Dower House
Crescent Place
Cheltenham
Gloucester GL50 3RA

The Countryside Commission for Scotland
Battleby
Redgorton
Perth PH1 3EW

Cumbria Tourist Board
Ashleigh
Holly Road
Windermere LA23 2AQ

East Anglia Tourist Board
Toppesfield Hall
Hadleigh
Suffolk IP7

East Midlands Tourist Board
Exchequergate
Lincoln LN2 1PZ

English Heritage
Keysign House
429 Oxford Street
London WIR 2HD

English Tourist Board
Thames Tower
Black's Road
London W6 9EL

The Forestry Commission
231 Corstorphine Road
Edinburgh EH12 7AT

Guild of Guide Lecturers
Grandma Lees Restaurant
2 Bridge Street
London SW1A 2JR

Heart of England Tourist Board
Woodside
Larkhill Road
Worcester WR5 2EQ

Heritage Education Trust
St Mary's College
Twickenham
Middlesex TW1 4SX

Highlands and Islands Enterprise Board
Bridge House
27 Bank Street
Inverness IV1 1QR

Historic Churches Preservation Trust
Fulham Palace
London SW6 6EA

Historic Houses Association
10 Charles II Street
London SW1Y 4AA

Historic Scotland
20 Brandon Street
Edinburgh EH3 5RA

Inland Waterways Association
114 Regent's Park Road
London NW1 8UQ

London Tourist Board
26 Grosvenor Gardens
London SW1W 0DU

Museums Association
34 Bloomsbury Way
London SC1A 2SF

Museums and Galleries Commission
7 St James Square
London SW1Y 4JU

The National Trust
36 Queen Anne's Gate
London SW1H 9AS

National Trust for Scotland
5 Charlotte Square
Edinburgh EH2 4DU

Northern Ireland Tourist Board
River House
48 High Street
Belfast BT1 2DS

Northumbria Tourist Board
Aykley Heads
Durham City
Durham DH1 5UX

Northumberland National Park
Eastburn
South Park
Hexham NE46 1BS

North West Tourist Board
Swan House
Swan Meadow Lane
Wigan Pier
Wigan WN3 5BB

The Royal Society for the Protection of Birds
The Lodge
Sandy
Bedfordshire SG19 2DL

Rural Development Commission
141 Castle Street
Salisbury SP1 3TP

Scottish Museums Council
County House
20–22 Torphichen Street
Edinburgh EH3 8JB

Scottish Tourist Board
23 Ravelston Terrace
Edinburgh EH4 3EU

Society for the Protection of Ancient Buildings
37 Spital Square
London E1 6DY

South East England Tourist Board
The Old Brew House
1 Warwick Park
Tunbridge Wells
Kent TN2 5TU

Southern Tourist Board
40 Chamberlayne Road
Eastleigh
Hampshire SO5 5JH

Thames and Chilterns Tourist Board
The Mount House
Church Green
Witney
Oxon OX8 6DZ

Tynedale Council (Hadrian's Wall Country)
Prospect House
Hexham NE46 3NH

Wales Tourist Board
Brunel House
2 Fitzalan Road
Cardiff CF2 1UY

West Country Tourist Board
60 St David's Hill
Exeter EX4 4SY

Yorkshire and Humberside Tourist Board
312 Tadcaster Road
York YO2 2HF

Index